1547- 1584

Ivan the Terrible

From an engraving by P. Veigel, end of the 16th century

TSAR IVAN IV THE TERRIBLE

S. F. PLATONOV

Ivan the Terrible

EDITED AND TRANSLATED BY

Joseph L. Wieczynski

WITH

IN SEARCH OF IVAN THE TERRIBLE
BY
Richard Hellie

ACADEMIC INTERNATIONAL PRESS

1974

THE RUSSIAN SERIES / Volume 28

S. F. Platonov **IVAN THE TERRIBLE**

Translation of *Ivan Groznyi* (Leningrad, 1923)

Library of Congress Catalog Card Number: 77-176468
ISBN: 0-87569-054-8
A Catalog Card follows the Index
Russian Series titles follow the Index

Printed in the United States of America

ACADEMIC INTERNATIONAL PRESS
Box 555   Gulf Breeze, Florida 32561

To the memory of my father
Joseph John Wieczynski
(1901-1970)

▨ Conquests during Ivan IV.	⊞ Losses during the Troubles.
▨ Losses during Ivan IV	⊟ Conquests during Alexis.

MUSCOVY IN THE 16th AND 17th CENTURIES

CONTENTS

From the *Book of Titles*

IVAN VASILIEVICH, TSAR AND GRAND PRINCE OF ALL RUSSIA

IN SEARCH OF IVAN THE TERRIBLE

RICHARD HELLIE

The reign of Ivan the Terrible has proved to be one of the most enduringly fascinating periods of Russian history. Relatively little documentary evidence survives from the years of Ivan's life—he was born in 1530 and reigned between 1547 and 1584—but enough is extant to permit the creation of an interesting narrative. S.F. Platonov's study sums up the pre-revolutionary knowledge of that era and represents a superb attempt to offer a rational explanation of the policies and actions of Ivan the Terrible.

Sergei Fedorovich Platonov (1860-1933) was the representative *par excellence* of the St. Petersburg school of Russian historiography. The members of this school based their historical interpretations on "facts" rather than on a broad understanding of the nature of the historical process. This school, some of whose other members were K.N. Bestushev-Riumin (1829-97), A.S. Lappo-Danilevsky (1863-1919), V.I. Sergeevich (1835-1911), A.E. Presniakov (1871-1929) and N.I. Kostomarov (1817-85), stands in contrast to the Moscow "state" historical school represented by K.D. Kavelin (1818-85) and B.N. Chicherin (1825-1904), and their successors S.M. Soloviev (1820-1879), V.O. Kliuchevsky (1841-1911) and P.N. Miliukov (1859-1943). The historians of the Moscow school tended to fit the facts to a broad framework of historical development initially derived from the theories of the German philosopher, G.F. Hegel. The latter approach to the writing of history was rejected

by the members of the St. Petersburg school, who refused
to fill in factual lacunae with guesses, and abstained from
the elaboration of grandiose historical schemes.

Sergei Platonov is perhaps most noted for two things:
his supervision of the publication of vast numbers of documents on early modern Russia, particularly in the *Russian
Historical Library*, and his monumental study, published in
1899, of the Time of Troubles. This turbulent period of
Russian history Platonov dated from the death of Ivan IV
in 1584 to the inauguration of the Romanov dynasty in
1613. Consequently his present study of Ivan the Terrible
serves as an historical prelude to his survey of the Time of
Troubles.

Platonov, the grandson of a serf, was born on June 16
(28) 1860. He completed studies at St. Petersburg University in 1882, and after 1889 he was a professor at this institution. There he directed the department of Russian history, succeeding his mentor, K.N. Bestuzhev-Riumin, an
historian with a positivist outlook, who had died two years
earlier. Although he was to become a leading light in the
St. Petersburg school of history, Platonov acknowledged the
influence of both Soloviev and Kliuchevsky in the formation of his own historical perceptions. Thus, like Soloviev
and Kliuchevsky, Platonov underscored the role of material
forces, geography and climate, in history, and he also stress-
ed the military role of the state. On the other hand, he
was not a determinist. Rather, he tended to de-emphasize
the place of moral forces in history. Himself fundamentally
 a positivist, he showed little interest in philosophies of history and found no interpretive role for the writer of history.
Instead he was concerned with determination of the scientific laws or regularities responsible for historical events. Like
the members of the state historical school, Platonov inclined
to view power, in this instance the monarchy, as the primary

agent in the constitution of society. When he set about studying the late sixteenth century, an era when various social classes appeared to prompt the state power, this orientation generated difficulties for him. It was also typical of Platonov that, while he accorded considerable attention to the personalities of rulers, he nonetheless joined many other Russian historians in taking little account of the complexities and subtleties of international relations.

In 1888 Platonov defended his master's dissertation, "Old Russian Tales and Stories about the Time of Troubles of the Seventeenth Century as an Historical Source." This work was published for the first time that same year. As his doctoral dissertation, Platonov in 1899 presented his magnificent "Essays on the History of the Time of Troubles in the Muscovite State in the Sixteenth and Seventeenth Centuries," which appeared in three editions prior to the Revolution, and again in 1937 in the Soviet Union. Platonov's major shorter but important historical writings were anthologized in *Articles on Russian History (1883-1912)*.

The most singular achievement of Platonov's career was his account of the Time of Troubles. The volume treating this era published in 1899 will remain a classic work of history. To contemporaries, however, perhaps Platonov was better known and more influential because of his textbooks. His *Textbook of Russian History*, used in secondary schools in Russia, saw many printings, and remained in use among Russian emigrés after the author's death. I myself have an edition published in Buenos Aires in 1945. An abridged English translation of this textbook was published in 1928, and reissued in 1964 by University Prints and Reprints (now Academic International Press). At present it continues in use at several American colleges and universities. Equally influential was *Lectures on Russian History*, read for a quarter century at St. Petersburg University and published in ten editions between 1899 and 1917. These popular textbooks, notwithstanding their strongly monarchist bent, helped to shape the outlooks of two generations of Russian students. Perhaps the influence of Platonov's propensity for factual presentation survives among the Leningrad historians of today. Their work remains notably less schematic and dogmatic than that of their Moscow counterparts, the successors of the ideological "state" historical school.

Platonov was honored by two Festschrifts: *To Sergei Fedorovich Platonov: Pupils, Friends, and Admirers* (1911; reprinted 1970) and *Collection of Articles on Russian History Dedicated to S.F. Platonov* (1922), which begins with a list of 98 of Platonov's works.

After the Revolution Platonov published a number of shorter works. Besides the work presented in translation here, issued in 1923, in 1921 he published a short biography, *Boris Godunov* (published 1973 in English translation by Academic International Press), treating a central figure in the Time of Troubles. Next, he wrote a transitional article on the development of serfdom with the title "On the Time and Measures of the Binding of Peasants to the Land in Muscovite Russia" (*Archive of the History of Labor in Russia*, 1922, Book 3). In this essay he attempted to reconcile the old "nondecree interpretation" of enserfment with recently discovered evidence pointing to active state involvement in this process. Then, in 1925, he published *Moscow and the West* (printed in English translation in 1972 by Academic International Press) wherein he discussed Russia's return to Western civilization in the sixteenth and seventeenth centuries, after the "detour to the East" during the era of Mongol conquest.

Even though he was a conservative monarchist, Platonov continued to hold important posts under the new Soviet government. He was head of the Archaeographic

Commission (1918-1929), director of the prestigious Pushkin House of the Academy of Sciences' Institute of Russian Literature (1925-29), and director of the library of the Academy of Sciences (1925-28). Ultimately these positions contributed to his downfall. Notwithstanding his prestige, Platonov was removed from his posts at the beginning of the Stalin Revolution. He was accused of illegally keeping archival materials of great state importance, including the Abdication Act of Nicholas II. Subsequently it was alleged that he had been part of a monarchist plot to overthrow Soviet power and place Grand Duke Andrei Vladimirovich on the Russian throne. The great literary critic and genius, R.I. Ivanov-Razumnik, reported seeing Platonov after his arrest. The dean of pre-Soviet historiography had been subjected to utter humiliation. Thereafter Platonov was exiled to Samara (now Küibyshev) on the Volga, where he died.

It should be mentioned that Platonov, while not considering himself a great literateur, was a master of the Russian language. The art of Platonov's writing style is not easily conveyed in translation. His lexicon was far richer, more varied and more specific than that of any Soviet historian of whom I am aware. In addition, his writing is distinguished by the frequent and telling inclusion of terms and phrases drawn from the period under examination. These are extremely difficult to render into modern Russian, not to say English. That the translator has succeeded so well in this treacherous task is a tribute to his skill.

In writing *Ivan the Terrible*, Platonov made exemplary use of the documentary evidence then available, and he relied heavily on primary sources. One of the major documents he employed was the "correspondence" between Tsar Ivan and a renegade military deserter, Prince Andrei Kurbsky. Platonov's text carries recurrent quotations from this exchange. Therefore the reader should be aware that

Edward Keenan of Harvard University, in his recent *The Kurbskii-Groznyi Apocrypha*, has endeavored to demonstrate that the "correspondence" between Ivan and Kurbsky is a forgery contrived between approximately 1623 and 1675 by several authors. If Keenan is right (according to R.G. Skrynnikov, a prominent student of Ivan's rule, the Keenan thesis lacks scientific substantiation), Platonov's extracts from the "correspondence" do not serve to illustrate what he thought they did. However, while Keenan seems to be on solid ground (although a computer study of the language of these materials would be desirable), as I have argued in a review in the *Journal of Modern History*, the exchange in question is not an essential source for Ivan IV's reign. To be sure, this correspondence brilliantly illuminated a dramatic conflict at a rich historical moment. But our image of that time and place will not be significantly altered by the demise of the correspondence. Most of what was cast into sharp relief by the fire of the exchange is still there, but is simply more troublesome to find without its light. Moreover, the "letters" of Ivan and Kurbsky ultimately may prove to be helpful secondary sources. Others, of course, may disagree with these judgments.

Because of the sparseness of primary sources, Ivan's reign always has been the object of diverse and essentially incompatible interpretations. All readers of Russian history should be aware of the varying conceptual approaches to this era of Russia's development, for interpretation is the essence of history. The rationality of Ivan's actions, particularly during his later life, and the role of his reign in Russian history, are the basic interpretive issues involved.

Arguments for the rationality of Ivan's actions were first advanced in the eighteenth century by V.N. Tatishchev (1686-1750). In scattered remarks that partially pre-modern

Russian historian drew parallels between Ivan and his own
contemporary, Peter the Great. Tatishchev justified Ivan's
policies on grounds that they strengthened monarchical
rule. Furthermore, he condemned as treason the actions
of some dissipated aristocratic magnates. The Oprichnina,
which began in 1565 as a separate court for Ivan IV with
its own army-sized palace guard and in time encompassed
half of the Muscovite state, Tatishchev viewed as a proper
instrument of state policy. Another historian, I.N. Boltin
(1735-92), noted that Ivan utilized the Oprichnina to liqui-
date the magnates' economic and political sources of power.
Writing in the nineteenth century, K.D. Kavelin perceived
Ivan's actions as having clearly objective causes. The Oprichnina, a corps of 6000 men, entailed an effort by the
tsar to create, on the basis of meritorious service and without regard for social status by birth, a group of servitors
loyal to him. This new group would replace the hereditary
aristocracy as the major political force in the Muscovite
state. The formation of the Oprichnina, according to Kavelin, completed a cycle in the Hegelian struggle between
the aristocracy and the state. Similarly, S.M. Soloviev observed the Oprichnina as a necessary stage in the process
of the long struggle between the clan, personified by the
aristocratic boyars, and the state, which, in the sixteenth
century, finally triumphed. Adhering to Hegel's principle
that all that is real is rational, Soloviev endorsed the despo-
tism of Ivan's reign, particularly the struggle of the tsar to
strengthen the new middle service class at the expense of
the old boyar class. Platonov's teacher, K.N. Bestuzhev-
Riumin, upheld views similar to those of Soloviev when
analyzing the role of the Oprichnina in the development
of state power.
     The first historian to find feudalism in Russia was
N.P. Pavlov-Silvansky (1869-1907), who observed that the

creation of the Oprichnina involved large-scale confiscations of the remnants of princely hereditary appanages. The political influence of the princes, as a consequence, was effectively undermined. Accordingly, Russia experienced an era of transition, moving away from feudal political fragmentation originating in the thirteenth century toward the formation of a state structured along class lines, beginning around the middle of the sixteenth century.

The appearance of Marxist historians in Russia in the years before the Revolution injected a newer although no less rationalist viewpoint into the study of sixteenth century Muscovy. N.A. Rozhkov (1868-1927), despite his shift of analytical focus away from what Marxists call the political superstructure toward the economic base, arrived nonetheless at views somewhat analogous to those of Pavlov-Silvansky. In Rozhkov's reckoning, there occurred during the second half of the sixteenth century the onset of the "gentry revolution," a transfer of power from the appanage nobility of princes and boyars to the mass of gentry. The Oprichnina comprised one of the episodes of this revolution, the origin of which was an economic crisis wherein a money economy crowded out the natural economy practised by the princes and boyars, and forced an end to feudal relationships.

The first dean of Soviet historical studies, M.N. Pokrovsky (1863-1932), proclaimed an even more startling thesis. He maintained that the natural economy supporting feudalism yielded to merchant capitalism, the political expression of which was autocracy. Accordingly, the Oprichnina was nothing less than an alliance of the bourgeoisie and the middle service class landholders. The alliance was the end product of a socio-political process begun long before Ivan, a process so mechanically inevitable and irresistible that the play of personalities and moralities as agents

of history pale in comparison. Regrettably, the simplici-
ties of this historical interpretation conceal a certain internal inconsistency. Were it true that the agrarian revolution,
the destruction of large patrimonial or manorial estates, was
completed in the first half of the sixteenth century, then
the Oprichnina was senseless, for it was assaulting an already powerless enemy. Pokrovsky further insisted that the
Oprichnina represented a gesture of self-defense by Tsar
Ivan, an interpretation which violated the author's Marxist
understanding of the impersonal causation of the historical
process. Trying to salvage something of his thesis by grasp-
ing at straws, Pokrovsky also attributed the Oprichnina to
Russia's failure in the Livonian War. The middle service
class (*dvoriane*), thwarted in its attempts to grab new lands
in the Baltic area, turned to the seizure of boyar lands.
Finally, echoing one of Platonov's ideas, Pokrovsky suggested that the Oprichnina also represented an endeavor
by the other partner in the alliance, the merchant bourgeoisie, to seize control of the trade routes to the West.

Soviet historians have continued to explain Ivan the
Terrible's policies and actions as rationally motivated, although with less élan than Pokrovsky. S.V. Bakhrushin
(1882-1950), I.I. Smirnov (1909-65), and R.I. Wipper
(1859-1954) all idealized Ivan and found in most of his
measures thoughtful steps necessary to the modernization
of Russia. A Soviet scholar writing today, A.A. Zimin,
continues this tradition in *Reforms of Ivan Groznyi* (1960)
and *The Oprichnina of Ivan Groznyi* (1964). The latter
work pictures the Oprichnina as needed to reinforce the
state against the threats to it posed by the appanage princes, Novgorod (an independent republic until the 1470's,
brutally sacked by Moscow's troops in 1570), and the
Church (many of whose leaders were executed).

Sergei Platonov's *Ivan the Terrible* should be read as part of this established and continuing tradition attributing rational causality and deliberate intent to Ivan's measures and their consequences. For Platonov, the Oprichnina represented a state reform coldly calculated to demolish the economic and political might of the descendants of the appanage princes (the hereditary rulers of what often amounted to no more than huge estates) and the boyars (the chief counsellors and agents of the monarch). Both of these groups formed a potential opposition to the centralizing propensities exhibited by Moscow and its autocrat, Ivan IV. To replace the old aristocracy as the beneficiaries and pillars on which to rest the new unitary state, the monarch relied upon the new middle service class, which provided most of the cavalry archers, the mainstay of the Muscovite army at this time, and the towns. The purpose of the Oprichnina was the political annihilation of the dangerous princely class by shattering its landholding, by replacing patrimonial forms of landownership (*votchina*) with landholding in return for state service (*pomestie*) as the primary means of supporting the expanding middle service class. Another aspect of this political reconstruction involved the secularization of church lands and their inclusion in the Oprichnina.

Yet an added reason for the creation of the Oprichnina may be found in Platonov's portrayal of the times of Ivan the Terrible. He accounted for this strange institution in part as Ivan's reaction to the usurpation of his rightful authority by the "chosen council" (*izbrannaia rada*). Platonov did not think that the "chosen council" was a regular institution, but rather the private circle of Ivan's wellwishers. Other historians have converted the "chosen council" into a formal institution, an unwarranted assumption, as has been shown by the American scholar A.M. Grobovsky.

In this instance the desire to invent an institution where none existed is similar to the attempt to create a "Boyar Council." The term "chosen council" is found only in Andrei Kurbsky's *History of Ivan IV*, a work which Edward Keenan is convinced is another seventeenth-century forgery. Be that as it may—the term is not necessary for Platonov—it was these people, Ivan's chosen advisers, who "set Ivan off" by their betrayal during his illness in 1553 when they swore fealty to his cousin, the appanage prince Vladimir A. Staritsky, instead of to his own infant son, Ivan. Yet, for Platonov, the entire matter of the "chosen council" was troublesome. Because he could not define precisely the aspirations of the members of the "chosen council," his analysis lacked complete scientific veracity. Dealing with imponderables such as the "chosen council" was nothing like confronting indisputable historical facts—the executions of princes and transfers of land to new holders. Despite such problems, the present translation is the most persuasive presentation available in English representing the rationalist interpretation of the reign of Ivan the Terrible.

But—isn't it also possible that the tyrant Ivan was in actuality a madman whose actions defy any rational accounting? Because of this very real possibility, some historians have pictured the actions and reign of Ivan the Terrible as the irrational, erratic rule of a pathologically afflicted individual. Always the positivist, Platonov in this late work remained convinced of Ivan's rationality. Still, the attentive reader will notice that he was at least modestly seduced by the pathological explanation.

The pathological interpretation of much of Ivan's behavior also originated in the eighteenth century. M.M. Shcherbatov (1733-90), an ardent defender of the gentry, condemned Ivan's autocracy and his replacement of the boyars in state administration by officials of non-noble descent. Shcherbatov looked upon Tsar Ivan's oppression of the boyars as a product of his unfounded suspicion of the nobility. Similar views were held by N.M. Karamzin (1766-1826), who observed that Ivan cut down boyars who did not oppose him and who always had been allied with the monarch. There were no plots against Ivan, and there could not have been, for they existed solely in the confused mind of the tsar.

Vasily O. Kliuchevsky (1841-1911), the best known nineteenth-century Russian historian, shared the pathological view of Ivan. He believed that the ruler, acting in the context of tensions between the autocracy and the aristocracy, had torn apart a social fabric which was becoming rewoven. The boyars did not threaten Ivan. Yet, acting like an obsessively frightened man, he destroyed the individuals he suspected of opposing him. In Kliuchevsky's reckoning, the Oprichnina was directed against men, not against the prevailing system, and consequently it was politically aimless. Nonetheless, the Oprichnina introduced anarchy and shook the very foundations of the Muscovite state.

For purposes of discussion and comparison, I shall try here to make an abbreviated but convincing case for the "pathological" interpretation. While Ivan's reign consisted of considerably more than the Oprichnina, I wish to focus mainly on that because it has become the axis of historiographic interest. Again, the reader will decide which interpretation is more tenable.

The Oprichnina was one of the most bizarre episodes in Russia's entire history. Created in 1565, within seven years it encompassed half of the territory of the Muscovite state, and included a palace guard of 6000 debauched adventurers who massacred thousands of people. In 1571 the Oprichnina army failed to prevent the Crimean Tatars from burning Moscow, while the following year the army of the Zemshchina (that part of Muscovy not a part of the Oprichnina) defeated the Tatars. Thereupon Ivan closed down the Oprichnina. Platonov, it should be mentioned, thought the Oprichnina was not closed until 1584, when Ivan died. In the observation of the Soviet historian S.B. Veselovsky (1876-1952), Platonov was misled by the fact that the records of the Oprichnina and Zemshchina were not integrated after the split ceased to exist in 1572.

Ivan's true interest in launching the Oprichnina remains obscure. If indeed this measure helped to consolidate the autocracy, it did so, according to R.G. Skrynnikov, the author of *The Beginning of the Oprichnina* (1966), *The Oprichnina Terror* (1969) and other studies, in ways which could not have been anticipated or planned. When initiatives are inserted into a functionally integrated national system, they often produce systemic consequences other than those immediately intended. So it was with the Oprichnina. It is difficult to understand why Ivan feared the old magnates. Institutionally, the officials were appointed by the ruler and served at his pleasure. They enjoyed only that official identity which the sovereign conferred upon them. Nor did they possess an organization of their own. The oft-cited "Boyar Council" (*Duma*) is the figment of the imagination of the nineteenth-century historians K.A. Nevolin (1806-55), N.P. Zagoskin (1851-1912), and V.O. Kliuchevsky, a myth still being perpetuated. As for the provincial princes, they were too busy struggling for place (*mestnichestvo*), power, and personal enrichment in Moscow to pose any collective threat to the monarch. Even during the political chaos of Ivan's minority (1533-47) no group or individual ventured to decentralize Muscovy or to diminish the institutional power of the monarchy. Moreover, it has been shown that neither the boyars nor the

princes were attacked as a class. Instead, only individuals
and families suffered at the hands of the oprichniki, and
some were themselves Oprichnina members. Survivors,
when there were any, recovered family properties after
1572. In addition, the Oprichnina seems not to have been
intended to create an autocratic monarchy based on the
middle service class cavalry archers. The evidence available indicates that more of the *pomestie* (service holding)
lands were confiscated for inclusion in the Oprichnina than
were *votchina* (patrimonial) estates belonging to the boyars
and princes. Moreover, many members of the middle service class were physically exterminated. As for the Church,
data now available show that Church landholding increased
in the years 1565-72.

In brief, that the Oprichnina was fundamentally a product of Ivan's warped mind is a thesis for which sufficient
evidence now exists. This offended Platonov's positivist
outlook, as it does even some historians today. The present work is replete with phrases hinting that Platonov
himself was not fully convinced by his own theory. He
noted that Ivan exhibited the attitude of a man in danger,
one who feared an imagined menace. There was no potential opposition to Ivan; as Platonov put it, his power was
not endangered. Ivan was suspicious, he surrendered to
fear and suspicion, and struck out at all who seemed hostile and dangerous—nobles, ordinary servicemen, churchmen, menials. His unceasing hunt for enemies who were
not resisting him inspired insane, unnecessary terror. Ty-
pically, in his testament of 1572, Ivan presented himself
as persecuted. Yet, notwithstanding these statements,
Platonov went no further than to declare that Ivan's condition did not develop into a clearly defined mental illness, that he was not insane.

Presumably, this attitude was based on Platonov's un-
willingness to grant the irrational full entry into history. It
rested also on what must have been a definition of insanity
considerably different from what would be countenanced
today. Platonov insisted that Ivan was capable of feeling
sincerely and of functioning physically. By insanity, therefore, he apparently meant a state of derangement in which
the afflicted foams at the mouth and is perpetually violent.

By more recent definitions of insanity, Ivan would
appear to have been a paranoid. The paranoid's basic pro-
cessing rule of thought is that whatever threat can be conceived is to be believed. Given the facts, it would be reasonable to characterize the Oprichnina as a madman's debauch. In this light the following behavior of Ivan the Terrible is more intelligible. In December 1564, Ivan left Moscow for Aleksandrova, where he ordered an enormous fortress built. Threatening to abdicate, he refrained from doing
so when the capital townsmen, agitated by Ivan's agents,
vowed to aid him in liquidating his enemies. When the tsar
returned to Moscow in February of 1565, there to proclaim
the Oprichnina and to execute and deport his "enemies,"
his beard and hair had fallen out.

R.G. Skrynnikov's works delineate the ever-widening
circles of Ivan the Terrible's suspicions and liquidations,
as one "case" led to another. Prior to the launching of
the Oprichnina at the beginning of the 1560's, Ivan's disgrace had fallen on Silvester and Adashev. Before 1560
these men had been leading members of the "chosen council." They were replaced by members of the Zakharin family of boyars, who soon lost Ivan's favor, and were followed
by Boyarin A.D. Basmanov, an old Moscow noble, who
launched a reign of terror against those Ivan suspected of
disloyalty. The old Moscow nobility, under Basmanov,
were Ivan's tools at the outset of the Oprichnina, when

the surviving members of the "chosen council" and the descendants of the princes of Vladimir-Suzdal were executed or exiled to Kazan province, a region on the Volga recently conquered from the Tatars. The leading member of the Vladimir-Suzdal nobility, A.B. Gorbatyi, had defended Silvester, as had other members of these ancient princely families. One of Gorbatyi's younger relatives, Prince A.I. Nokhtev, went to serve in the Staritsky appanage, perhaps to escape from the oprichniki. Although, in 1566, those who had survived exile to Kazan were allowed to return and given back their now irretrievably devastated estates, the economic power of these princes was effectively undercut.

When the Assembly of the Land, a parliament-like body, was convoked in summer 1566 to discuss the seemingly endless Livonian War (1558-1583), some of its members demanded an end also to the Oprichnina and to its terrorism. For their trouble, some of the protestors were executed. Evidently this and other protests heightened Ivan's suspicions, provoking him to set in motion a second phase of the Oprichnina. The landed areas of this state within a state were expanded and so was the size of the corps of oprichniki. Ivan built for himself a new castle in Moscow in 1567 and took residence there. Simultaneously, should his new keep fail him, Ivan ordered over ten thousand workmen to build a stone fortress in remote Vologda, where five hundred arquebusiers stood guard day and night. He relocated his treasury there. Obviously influenced by the Varangian legend of the origin of the Riurikid dynasty told in the earliest chronicles, Ivan related to foreign visitors that he was a stranger ruling subject peoples and might be forced to flee. For that eventuality, he directed the construction of a fleet of boats in Vologda as a means of escaping to England. On the other hand, like the Russian he was, Ivan also bestowed the large sum of 200 rubles on

the Monastery of St. Cyril in Beloozero to pay for the
building of a private cell for himself should he desire to
become a monk. In aggregate, these acts hardly seem
those of a person in full possession of his faculties.

Perhaps Ivan's talk of abdicating led to discussion
of a successor. This was the background against which
the "Staritsky plot" evolved. Prince V.A. Staritsky had
been the candidate chosen to succeed Ivan during the
latter's illness in 1553. Staritsky remained a logical
choice during the era of the Oprichnina. For whatever
reason, the unfortunate Staritsky was arrested, and later
executed with other members of his family in October
1569. (The prince himself was compelled to drink poison.) Apparently, while in custody, he denounced I.P.
Fedorov, a powerful personage with the high rank of
Equerry, who had befriended early victims of the Oprichnina by providing bail for them. Fedorov was murdered by the Oprichnina in September 1568.

Somewhat earlier, in a sermon delivered in March
1568, Metropolitan Filipp Kolychev, who had been advanced to his post as head of the Russian Orthodox
Church thanks to the support of his relatives, the Zakharins, called for the curtailment of repressions. In return, he was tried on fabricated charges, removed from
his post, and incarcerated in a monastery. Then came
the turn of Novgorod. In this "case" the central figure,
Boyarin V.N. Danilov, had been an associate of Equerry
I.P. Fedorov. The oprichniki descended on Novgorod
in 1570 to execute Danilov and all linked to him. As
many as 4000 perished in this pogrom alone. Disturbed,
Archbishop Pimen of Novgorod, who had collaborated
with the authorities earlier in the trial of the Metropolitan Filipp, made his feelings known, and was repaid with
accusations of treason. The Oprichnina leader, Basmanov,

refused to participate in the Novgorod terror, for which in-
discretion he was denounced for complicity with Pimen.
Other prominent individuals, including most of the previous
leaders of the Oprichnina, were linked to the "Novgorod
treason case," and executed in July 1570. The purging of
the purgers in summer 1570 signalled the third and last
phase of the Oprichnina, which was closed two years later,
after the 1571 failure of the Oprichnina army to defend
Moscow from a Tatar sacking, and in the following year
the defeat of the Tatars on the Molody river by the Zemshchina army, evidently induced Ivan to terminate it. But
the riot of bloodletting had not run its full course. Later
Ivan resumed his antics, and in September or October 1575
temporarily renounced the throne in favor of a Tatar of
Kasimov, Simeon Bekbulatovich, and himself became, nominally, a mere appanage prince of Moscow. This farce, replete with executions as Ivan again feared for his life, lasted
eleven months. The last victim of the killing can be considered to be Ivan's own son, the seventeen-year-old Tsarevich, Ivan Ivanovich. His principal adviser had been a
Zakharin, who may have planted discord between father
and son and, wittingly or not, brought on the murder in
1581 of the son by the father.

Like Stalin's terrorism and purges, the Oprichnina was
a product of a tyrant's paranoia. It destroyed individuals
feared by the ruler but only incidentally changed, and then
in unintended and relatively minor ways, established political institutions. Although the investigation department of
the Oprichnina, under Maliuta Skuratov and V. Griaznoi,
manufactured the later and most heinous "cases," it was
Ivan who ordered the investigations, believed the results,
and took vengeance on the accused. It was he who ordered entire families exterminated, knowing that more than
death itself Muscovites feared not having anyone to offer

prayers for the dead. Thereupon Ivan sent to monasteries lists of thousands of victims, together with cash offerings for the saying of the prayers for the souls of the deceased.

From available evidence it is reasonable to conclude that Ivan was a classic paranoid. That the "correspondence" between Ivan and Kurbsky possibly no longer can be considered a primary source is unfortunate, for it is heavy with relevant testimony. Even so, as a secondary source, it serves to illustrate what the seventeenth century considered to be a plausible portrait of Ivan. The evidence cited here, together with that on record elsewhere, demonstrates that Ivan made erroneous judgments about threats to him posed by others, dangers which did not correlate to experience. This is the basic feature of paranoia, a disorder of middle age (35-50). Ivan was 35 to 42 years of age at the time of the Oprichnina. Paranoia frequently occurs after the death of a spouse, as seems true in Ivan's case. The sadism, debauchery, and sexual abuse institutionalized in the years 1565-1572 suggest erotomaniac expressions of paranoia. Today the disorder seems to afflict particularly the more intelligent, more educated elements of society. The impressions of Ivan gained by numerous foreigners picture a highly intelligent, knowledgeable individual. Obviously, Tsar Ivan suffered most severe delusions of persecutions and, correspondingly, he was intensely hostile, vigilant, and suspicious.

It is a matter of record that Ivan repeatedly accused of treason men to whom once he had been very attached. These he attacked in anticipation that they might strike at him. Furthermore, the tsar's condemnation of the refusal of the magnates to swear fealty to his infant son during his illness in 1553, a rational decision from their point of view, might be termed a disordered retrospective falsification. To these paranoid characteristics should be added the clear signs that Ivan suffered delusions of grandeur (perhaps not always of his own making). These he displayed after his coronation in 1547. They ranged from willing inheritance of the mantle of God's earthly viceregent to his claim in diplomatic exchanges of descent from the mythical Prus. The centralizing of all of Russia's cultural traditions in Moscow certainly must have fed these aspects of Ivan's paranoid tendencies. Equally indicative of his infirm mental state was his craving of praise and recognition (for example, his threatened abdication) and his hypersensitivity to criticism (execution of critics of the Oprichnina). Together these psychological characteristics strongly suggest profound feelings of inadequacy, which came out in Ivan's apparently sincere thoughts of becoming a monk. Finally, like the typical paranoid, Ivan utilized the devices and institutions of his day in achieving his bizarre wishes. Some examples of this were his abdication, the establishment of a state within a state, his playing on the popular image of the monarch, his temporal role and popular authority.

To turn for a moment to the operation of the Oprichnina, headed by Ivan as its lord, it should be understood that this institution did not in reality supplant or even duplicate the state administrative network. It did include certain administrative bodies and officials: palace court offices and their administrators, a treasury, a keeper of the seal, and regional tax chancelleries (*cheti*) for revenue gathering. P.A. Sadikov (1891-1942) showed that the *cheti* were organized to collect the old "feeding" (*kormlenie*) revenues which had been paid to the centrally-appointed provincial governors (*namestniki*) until abolished in 1555-1556. Then, for a brief interval, according to the Leningrad historian N.E. Nosov, the right to collect these monies was sold for a flat fee to the provincial taxpayers themselves. The creation of the regional tax chancelleries was one of many

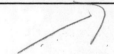

steps in the second half of the sixteenth century in the direction of the establishment of central, specialized bureaux
in Moscow, and was in accord with the historical development of the period. Thus there was nothing extraordinary
in this innovation. In fact, given the generally predatory
nature of the Oprichnina, it is hardly surprising that its sole
institutional innovation was connected with a form of popular exploitation, taxation. With this exception, few if any
administrative reforms were introduced by the Oprichnina,
nor were changes made in the order or manner of government, diplomacy, or foreign policy. Using primarily medieval forms, the Oprichnina may be understood as a state
within, or over, a state, at the beginning of the early modern era.

In contrast, senior boyars headed the Zemshchina and
inherited, or rather continued, most of Muscovy's regular
administrative machinery as it existed in 1564. These offices and officials, all directly subservient to the monarch,
comprised the Treasury, the Keeper of the Seal, the Moscow Administrative-Judicial Chancellery, the Service Land
Chancellery, the Robbery Chancellery, the Great Revenue
Chancellery. The existing Foreign Affairs and Military
chancelleries continued to function, in the Zemshchina,
for both segments of Muscovy. Apparently a single Post
Chancellery, the marvel of Western visitors to Muscovy,
operated as usual. A joint Robbery Chancellery existed
to prosecute felons when one party was subject to Zemshchina administration, the other to the Oprichnina.

There were several important ways in which this
incredible product of Ivan's diseased imagination sapped
the strength of Muscovy. It is clear that the Oprichnina
debauch contributed to Moscow's conspicuous lack of
success in the Livonian War. More telling was the blow
the Oprichnina (in conjunction with the Livonian War)

delivered to Muscovy's productive capacities and general
level of economic development, which the late Soviet historian D.P. Makovsky termed, perhaps with some exagger-
ation, "pre-capitalism." Furthermore, enserfment advanced both during and as a consequence of the Oprichnina.
The last remaining peasant free holdings ("black lands")
in the Moscow region were assigned to oprichniki as service land grants, abasing the affected peasant. Worse, the
oprichniki were granted, or perhaps usurped, the right to
treat and tax peasants in any way they pleased. This contributed further to their abasement. The dislocations produced by Oprichnina depredations caused crop failures and
epidemics, and stimulated peasant flight. Engendered thereby was the intense competition for peasant tenants that
marked the last years of Ivan's reign. This scarcity of labor was a primary cause of the introduction in 1581 of the
Forbidden Years, a restriction which abrogated the long-
established right of peasants to leave the service of a landholder or owner on St. George's Day. These developments,
accelerating markedly the progress of enserfment, flowed
from the Oprichnina, even though they were by no means
what Ivan had intended in January of 1565.

Still a further result of the Oprichnina was the exter-
mination of many princes and boyars, fated to be included
among Ivan's "enemies." Their already quite limited influence now further diminished. Such collective power as
they had exerted institutionally as nearly exclusive counsellors of the ruler was undermined as well by the eleva-
tion of a few lowly-born state secretaries (*diaki*) to the
rank of counsellor state secretaries (*dumnye diaki*). The
withering of the power of the princes and boyars may have
been counterbalanced by a slight rise of that of the cavalry
archers of the middle service class (see my *Enserfment and
Military Change in Muscovy* for greater detail).

Central to the pathological interpretation of Ivan the Terrible's reign is a full appreciation of the milieu which permitted the flowering of so many bizarre happenings. First, there were few other than certain natural restraints, such as geography, tradition, and perhaps kinship structure, on the Muscovite monarch. Continuing to use the terminology of political science, there were almost no direct restraints on the Russian monarchy: there was no constitution, no tradition of the rule of law. One may attempt to explain this, and particularly the seemingly total absence of indirect, or institutional, restraints, by noting that Russia did not experience those aspects of feudalism which in the West gave birth to ideas about the pluralistic and autonomous access of different groups to the major attributes of social, cultural, and political life. In Muscovy there were no city states, and the Russian medieval political tradition did not bequeath to the sixteenth century a feeling of dichotomy between state and society. Early Russia did not develop notions of an autonomous class society or the class consciousness characteristic of Western Europe. The state tended to dominate society. These factors contributed to and were expressed in the absence of indirect restraints on Ivan the Terrible.

The Church could not restrain the monarch, for it had been the state's handmaiden for most of the time since its introduction in 988, the date of the conversion of Russia to Christianity. Ivan removed with ease any clergyman, including the head of the Church himself, the metropolitan, who opposed his actions.

The nobility was incapable of uniting to resist the undertakings of the ruler. Professor Gustave Alef has demonstrated that a population explosion had so swelled the number of aristocrats and, because of the practice of dividing inheritances equally, had so reduced their estates in size that, hat in hand, as a matter of survival they besieged Moscow, begging posts. The system of places according to birth and rank (*mestnichestvo*) kept the nobles at each other's throats, fighting for place, post, and spoils. It is nearly certain that no "Boyar Council" existed which might have checked the monarch. The boyars themselves were no more than the tsar's creatures. The administration of the Muscovite state, which incorporated executive, legislative, and judicial functions in one organization with one head, while just emerging from and still retaining many characteristics of a palace household, naturally was a malleable tool in the hand of its head, the tsar.

It should be remembered also that there was no gentry which could coalesce against autocratic caprice. The middle service class was not a gentry in the conventional understanding of that term, but rather a group of 17,500 men of varying and often indifferent social origin who served at the behest of the monarch. Only so long as they served did they hold their service lands (*pomestie*). Moreover, this group of cavalry militia was of comparatively recent origin, forming at the end of the fifteenth century. Reforms adopted during Ivan's reign allotted to them considerable authority in local provincial administration. But little glory for these servitors from the periphery and even less influence on the center derived from this authority. Prior to Ivan's new arrangements, local administration was the province of centrally directed provincial officials (*volosteli, tiuny*). Nearly all of these officers were slaves belonging to the governors (*namestniki*) appointed from Moscow. Consequently, the middle service class *dvoriane* and *deti boyarskie* assumed posts recently held by slaves. Although it is true that these had been slaves with comparatively high prestige, nevertheless they cannot have bequeathed to their successors a tradition of standing up to the central authority. Not until the middle service class acquired some of the status and prerogatives once limited to the upper service class boyars and princes did it dare attempt to improve its standing. But this did not take place until the first half of the seventeenth century when the monarchy was shaken by a vast social crisis. In Ivan's day the middle servitors lacked status and power, and their loyalties were well enough known by the Oprichnina investigation chancellery that they could be sorted out for service as oprichniki or in the Zemshchina.

Apart from the absence of direct and indirect restraints on his will, Ivan the Terrible possessed another source of power. This was the grip he had on the popular imagination of Muscovy. As monarch he enjoyed among the Russian people the sacred image of God's earthly regent, one who spoke with divine authority. And on this theme Ivan played brilliantly. For example, when he journeyed to Aleksandrova to begin the Oprichnina, ostensibly Muscovy was left without government. Contrary to custom, a group of boyars was not named to govern in the absence of the sovereign. The people of Russia, awed by the image of the Muscovite sovereigns built up by certain church officials since 1500, cowed in terror and, in the words of a chronicler, pleaded: "How can sheep be without a shepherd?" The establishment of the Oprichnina remedied this want. The popular notion of the autocrat as the wise and protective shepherd rendered Muscovy's population inert and passive, and allowed Ivan to practice unprecedented official barbarism. He, like his modern counterpart, Stalin, experienced little difficulty in finding a handful of savages—Basmanov, Skuratov and Griaznoi, the Muscovite counterparts of Yezhov, Yagoda, Beria and Poskrebyshev of the

1930s and 1940s—who organized thugs and cutthroats (Stallin's NKVD cannibals were nicknamed oprichniki) to terrorize and brutalize all suspected of disloyalty by their paranoid master.

The pathological interpretation here argued should be compared with Platonov's claim that the Oprichnina was not "a senseless venture of a half-witted tyrant." By carefully reading this excellent translation the student of history can gain stimulating insights into the relative significance of geographical, institutional, and personal factors in the pageant of sixteenth-century Muscovy.

Ivan has been of recent interest not only to historians. The Soviet Ministry of Health publication *Forensic Medicine* (*Sudebno-meditsinskaia ekspertiza*, 1969, No. 1; 1970, No. 2) reported on a recent temporary exhumation of Ivan's body from its limestone coffin in the Cathedral of the Archangel in the Moscow Kremlin by a special commission of the USSR Ministry of Culture to conduct anthropological and chemical-toxicological, as well as historical, studies. Ivan had been buried in the woollen garb of a monk. His skull was small, with a strongly developed relief, a low brow and significantly projecting eyebrow region and chin. Judging by the skeleton, Ivan the Terrible was about five feet ten inches tall and must have possessed great physical strength. With the exception of a strongly pronounced proliferation of osteophytes, no pathological changes were manifested in Ivan's bones. The arsenic level was very low in Ivan's bones, so obviously he had never been poisoned with that. The amount of lead was relatively high, probably due to natural accumulation in the course of aging. The level of mercury was also comparatively high, perhaps connected with the use of medicines containing it; the possibility of acute and chronic mercury poisoning from the use of these preparations cannot be ruled out, the commission decided.

University of Chicago

PREFACE

JOSEPH L. WIECZYNSKI

Platonov's *Ivan Groznyi* is a well conceived attempt to pursue a simple objective, that of clarifying the motivation of Ivan the Terrible in his political work and of elucidating the influences that caused his reign to assume its peculiar political nature. Although recent scholarship has broadened and deepened our understanding of Ivan and his policies, Platonov's essay remains of great value to students of Ivan's reign. For in this work Ivan's personality, his biases and his motives emerge with a definition and a clarity rather unique in historiography. It must be admitted that throughout these pages we encounter little of the color, imagery and style that make Platonov's *Moscow and the West* and his work on the Time of Troubles such interesting and vivid literary accomplishments. Conceived and completed during the early years of Soviet rule in Russia, this book reflects something of the turmoil and uncertainty through which its author and all Russia were passing. Probably it is remarkable that its author, who soon was to suffer dislocation and banishment, was able to complete his manuscript at all, for momentous events can easily strangle creativity. Yet the starkness of Platonov's style and the bluntness of his exposition well suit the directness of his intention. In the end we are left with an interpretation of Ivan's accomplishments that divests his actions of much of the confusion, contradiction and mystery with which they have often been invested by

lesser historians. Against the background of current controversy concerning Ivan and the sources for the study of his
administration, this book should be of particular importance.
My chief concern in translating this work has been fidelity to the meaning of its author. Considerations of style
and niceties of expression have been subordinated to this
purpose wherever necessary. In editing this essay I have adhered to the same principles followed in my earlier rendi-
tion of Platonov's *Moscow and the West* (which was also
published by Academic International Press in 1972). I have
attempted to reduce my own explanations and commentar-
ies to a minimum, assuming in the reader a fundamental acquaintance with the history and institutions of Muscovite
Russia. Often I have retained in their original Russian form
terms that refer to lesser known Russian institutions and organizations. Such terms are defined by explanatory notes
upon their initial appearance in the text. Poorly known
personalities are identified similarly. Occasionally I rely upon internal editing to clarify Platonov's meaning. At such
times I supply more complete names for individuals Platonov cites only by surname, include dates for important events
and introduce similar illustrative material. I have followed
the generally accepted practice of dividing Platonov's longer
paragraphs and sentences into segments more in keeping
with English usage. All parenthetical material that appears
in this work is the author's. My own few intrusions into
the text are included within brackets. The system of trans-
literation is basically that of the Library of Congress, with
modifications. Ligatures are omitted. The initial Russian
diphthongs are rendered as "ya" and "yu," not as "ia" and
"iu." Usually the Russian soft sign is omitted when it pre-
cedes a vowel (e.g., *diaki*) or changed to "i" (e.g., *pomestie*).
The endings of proper Russian names are given as "y," not
as "i" or "ii."

Many friends and associates have assisted me not only
in producing this work but throughout my professional career. Professor Cyril Toumanoff, formerly of Georgetown
University and now historian of the Order of Malta in Rome,
first enkindled my interest in early Russian history by his
brilliant lectures, which have become legend among his former students. Professor Olgerd P. Sherbowitz-Wetzor of
Georgetown University, who has enriched generations of
students of Russia by his work on the Russian Primary
Chronicle, imparted to me something of his own love for
early Russian manuscripts. His death in 1970 was a sad
loss to many friends and colleagues. Professor Thomas T.
Helde, Father Frank Fadner and Father John Songster, all
of Georgetown, guided me through my apprenticeship as
an historian and have assisted me in many ways thereafter.
Mrs. Wolter J. Fabrycky of Blacksburg, Virginia offered
many valuable suggestions on the interpretation and translation of difficult passages in the original. Professor Peter
von Wahlde first aroused my interest in this project and
has offered numerous criticisms that have improved my
efforts. The American Philosophical Society and Virginia
Polytechnic Institute and State University have afforded
me several grants which made it possible for me to consult Russian sources throughout the United States. Mr.
Albert Graham, curator of the Slavic Room of the Library
of Congress, secured needed material for me and placed at
my disposal his rich knowledge of bibliographic and reference aids. Mrs. Carolyn Alls and Mrs. Diane Williams of the
Department of History of Virginia Polytechnic Institute and
State University typed parts of the manuscript and have assisted me in ways too numerous to mention. Professor
Richard Hellie of the University of Chicago has not only
enriched this work by his original introduction but has suggested many valuable emendations of the translation and

annotations. Professor Robert O. Crummey of Yale University kindly offered to investigate some of the troublesome references in Platonov's text. Mistakes that remain are the result of my own obstinacy. In identifying Russian terminology I am greatly indebted to the invaluable aid compiled by Sergei G. Pushkarev, *Dictionary of Russian Historical Terms from the Eleventh Century to 1917* (New Haven, 1970).

Once again my wife, Jo, has proved to be my most indispensable associate and collaborator. Her patience in reading and editing the manuscripts is matched only by the graciousness with which she has tolerated a husband who has disappeared for weeks on end into the depths of early Russian history. Without her assistance and her encouragement this work could never have been completed.

Virginia Polytechnic Institute
and State University

S · F · PLATONOV

the Ivan Terrible

CHAPTER I

IVAN THE TERRIBLE IN RUSSIAN HISTORIOGRAPHY

An entire book would be needed to review in detail what has been written about Ivan the Terrible by historians and poets. From Prince Mikhail Shcherbatov's *History of Russia* to R.Yu. Wipper's *Ivan Grozny*,[1] our knowledge of Ivan and his times has passed through a number of stages and has realized great success. It can be said that this success marks one of the brightest pages in the history of our scholarship and stands as one of the decisive victories of the scientific method. The author hopes that the following pages will make this statement sufficiently evident.

The main difficulty one faces when studying the era of Ivan the Terrible and his personal character and significance is not the complexity of the period and that of its central figure, but the great lack of material needed for such study. The turbulence of the Time of Troubles and the famous Moscow fire of 1626[2] destroyed so many Muscovite archives and ancient documents that the events of the sixteenth century must be studied from odd remnants and scraps of written material. Those not conversant with the methods of historical work probably would be amazed if told that a biography of Ivan the Terrible cannot be written, for we know extraordinarily little of the man himself. Biographies and descriptions of Peter the Great and his father, Tsar Alexis, can be written because these interesting individuals have left us their manuscripts: their official papers, notes, correspondence—in a word, their archives. But

nothing of the sort has come down to us from Ivan. We
do not know his handwriting, nor do we have so much as
a scrap of paper written by him. All the efforts of the eminent archaeographer, N.P. Likhachev,[3] to discover such a
fragment and to identify a single line of his writing came
to nothing. This careful researcher limited himself to pub-
lishing two brief inscriptions "without making assumptions,"
as he put it, and let it be known that he was willing to regard one of them a facsimile of Ivan's handwriting.[4]

We have none of the original texts of the literary
works attributed to Ivan, only their copies; and from these
we cannot reconstruct exactly the author's own text. Tsar
Ivan's famous "Epistle" to Prince Andrei Kurbsky[5] in 1564
reads differently in its various editions and copies, and we
cannot be certain which edition and which copy must be
considered the original. The same can be said of all the
other "works" attributed to Ivan. Even Ivan's "Testament"
of 1572, which is an official document, is not extant in its
original form but has been reprinted from an incomplete
and defective copy of the eighteenth century. If a learned
skeptic were to appear and contend that all of Ivan's
"works" were spurious, it would be difficult to argue with
him. We would have to prove Ivan's authorship through internal evidence, for the documents themselves fail to confirm it. The sole exception is Ivan's correspondence with
one of his favorites, Vasily Grigorievich Griazny-Il'in.[6]
When Griazny was captured by the Crimean Tatars, Ivan
"graciously" began to correspond with him concerning his
ransom. In time the texts of the Tsar's letters and those
of Griazny were included in the official record of "Crimean Affairs" and can therefore be regarded as true documents, an exact and authentic copy of their correspondence. For this reason the Tsar's exchange of letters with
Griazny has been accorded unusual historical significance,

as the most recent scholar to study these matters, P.A. Sadikov,[7] has correctly concluded.

So it is with Ivan's personal writings and letters. Yet
little more can be said for the entire body of chronicle material dealing with this era. In the sixteenth century the
writing of chronicles in Russia came under official control;
for this reason the chronicles become reserved and biased.
The official chroniclers either depersonalized the particular
archival records that they used or else altered them to suit
their needs. They strictly adhered to the government's
point of view when recording events that occurred in their
day. Often these chronicles were somewhat revised to re-
flect Tsar Ivan's attitudes, as can be seen from the so-called
Litsevoi svod.[8] The thirteenth volume of the *Complete Collection of Russian Chronicles* contains fragments from several pages of this collection that apparently have been revised and augmented at Ivan's personal command. Clearly the
historian who uses such a source must be extremely cautious, lest he fall victim to a one-sided interpretation of
events. But the same danger threatens the historian from
the other side as well. The Tsar and his official chroniclers described events in Moscow in their own fashion.
But so, too, did Ivan the Terrible's political enemies.

The notorious Prince A.M. Kurbsky fled to Lithuania
to escape the terror in Moscow and there composed his
History of the Grand Prince of Moscow. This work, a
very learned lampoon, was intended to influence public
opinion in Lithuania. It contains much historical material that is valuable and exact; therefore all of Kurbsky's
biased attacks upon Ivan acquire special force. Yet for all
that it remains a lampoon, not history, and we cannot accept the word of its author.

The accounts of Ivan provided by foreigners are yet
more biased. The clearest example of this is the "epistle"

written by the Livonians, Taube and Kruse,[9] on the "unprecedented tyranny of the Grand Prince of Moscow."
Even that learned and discreet Englishman, Giles Fletcher,[10]
in Moscow five years after Ivan's death, did not escape the
general mood of the times, which attributed to the dead
Muscovite tyrant personal guilt for all the disorder in Russian life at that time.

bias of sources

The historian who works with the chronicle material
and literary accounts from Ivan's era must exercise special
caution and should be prepared not only for pure subjec-
tivity but for passionate bias in every source that he con-
sults. Even when working with the literature of those
times he finds himself on uncertain ground. Bitter social
and political strife set its stamp upon everything. Ivan's
contemporaries directed their literary efforts toward the
urgent problems of the moment; but the primitive state
of their political consciousness prevented them from understanding and passing firm and clear judgments on these
matters. In all the "debates," "epistles," "denunciations,"
"petitions" and "tales" of the period the scholar searches
in vain for definite conceptions and programs. He encounters only a vague babble and obscure allusions to reality,
allusions made still more incomprehensible and suspect by
the ignorance of the copyists of these works. The literature of this era, like the historical sources, fails to offer the
historian much in the way of interpretation, nor does it
provide him the purely objective facts he needs to create
his own interpretation of the times.

Since this is the state of the historical materials, it is
clearly impossible to compose a serious and factually complete biography of Ivan the Terrible. It is worth our while
to recall what we actually do know of the various years of
Ivan's life. We shall remember that there are a number of
years of Ivan's life for which we have no information at all.

For example, there are no data concerning the earliest years of his life, except for three or four references in the letters of Ivan's father, Grand Prince Vasily, written to Ivan's mother, Elena Vasilievna, in 1530-1533. The Grand Prince was away and was concerned about the health of his first-born, "because about Friday Ivan became ill;" that is, "there appeared on his son Ivan's neck, right under the back of his head, a large, hard spot." The infant's abscess healed safely, and thereafter until the thirteenth year of his life we know nothing of his health or of his life in general.

At the end of 1543 the orphaned thirteen-year old sovereign first displayed his temper. He arrested one of the most distinguished boyars,[11] Prince Andrei Shuisky, and "ordered him to be turned over to the kennel keepers, and the kennel keepers seized and killed him." "And from that time," the chronicle observes, "the boyars began to fear the Sovereign." Yet nothing further is known of the doings of the young Grand Prince until 1547. During that year Ivan married and exchanged the title of Grand Prince for that of Tsar.[12] Then another dark interval follows until 1549. During the years 1549-1552 Ivan passed laws and waged war. In 1553 he fell gravely ill and quarreled with his boyars; and "from that time there was enmity between the Sovereign and his people." The second half of the 1550s again grows dark, and we know nothing of Ivan's personal life. We know a little only about his policy toward Livonia and of the beginning of war with that country. In 1560 Ivan's first wife died, and Ivan himself underwent something of a change in personality.

Accounts of the last years of Ivan's life are filled with tales of his atrocities and of the terror of the oprichnina. But these accounts are almost exclusively the work of foreigners and Kurbsky. Russian sources remain silent and limit themselves to brief observations, such as that in 1574 "the Tsar put to death in Moscow, on the Prechistaia Square in the Kremlin, many boyars, the archimandrite of the Chudov Monastery, an archpriest and many people of various ranks, and cast their heads into the court of Mstislavsky."[13] But all these tales and references are contradictory and quite imprecise. It is difficult to date them, and they give rise to many misunderstandings, such as those of which one reads in the works of Karamzin and later historians.[14] And there are few documents. Even the decree on the founding of the oprichnina has not come down to us in its original form.

Thus it is impossible to reconstruct an exact chronology or an authentic, factual account of the activities and personal life of Ivan the Terrible. The historian encounters series of years without a single reliable reference to Ivan himself. What sort of "biography" can be written under such circumstances? Where does one find the material for a proper evaluation of his character? Under such circumstances one can only venture conjectures that are more or less plausible and that more or less conform to the testimony of the meagre material that has survived.

An eighteenth-century historian, Prince M.M. Shcherbatov, in his *History of Russia*, "having studied the history of this sovereign," came to the conclusion that Ivan "seems to have so many sides that he often appears to have been more than one man." Captivated by the contradictions of his sources, this historian transferred those contradictions to the character of his hero. He found it impossible to refrain from guesses and deductions in his attempt to explain some of Ivan's personal qualities. He remarked of Ivan, not without wit, that "he who bears autocratic power and yet is also timid and base in character necessarily breeds anger, distrust and grim vengeance." Beyond this Shcherbatov would not venture. Having indicated Ivan's shortcomings, he contrasted them with his "shrewd and far-seeing intelligence" and saw in this anomaly the internal contradiction and duality of Ivan's character. In his *History of the Russian State* Karamzin expressed the same view of Ivan, albeit with greater literary skill. He was fascinated by the idea of describing the age in which Ivan lived. "What a glorious character for an historical portrait!" he wrote of Ivan to Nikolai Turgenev. The somber drama of those times struck Karamzin as entertaining from the literary point of view, and he depicted it with great artistic effect. But, like Shcherbatov, he failed to capture Ivan's character, even though he, too, tried to understand him "through speculation." "Despite all attempts at speculation," Karamzin wrote in his *History*, "the character of Ivan, who was a model of virtue in his youth and a vicious blood-sucker during the years of his manhood and old age, is a riddle to the mind."

Karamzin attempted to solve this riddle by relying upon Kurbsky's interpretation that Ivan always lacked intellectual independence and surrendered to the influence of those around him. He was virtuous when "he was guided by his pair of chosen favorites—Silvester and Adashev," but declined morally when he drew closer to depraved favorites. He appears to have been "a mixture of good and evil" and combined seemingly incompatible qualities: "a first-rate intellect" and a "rare memory" with the savageness "of a tiger" and "shameless slavishness toward the most vile lusts." Although Karamzin constantly lashes out at the contradictions in Ivan's nature, he nevertheless fails to supply the key to explaining these contradictions and leaves the riddle unsolved in his own mind. His portrayal of a subservient sovereign who was susceptible to outside influences would have been complete, had Karamzin admitted in his work that Ivan had been an intellectual

non-entity. But this he could not do, for Ivan always impressed him as "the phantom of a great monarch" who was "energetic," "untiring" and "often shrewd."
Karamzin set forth his "riddle" with remarkable picturesqueness and eloquence. Under his artistic pen Ivan's era came to life and was read with great enthusiasm. It was natural that others, using the material presented in Karamzin's *History*, should attempt to construct an even more realistic and subtle depiction of Ivan than that presented by Karamzin himself. The Moscow Slavophiles made such an attempt during their discussions of Ivan's character within their literary circle.[15] The fruit of their judgments Konstantin Aksakov and Yury Samarin committed to print.[16] In his work on Stefan Yavorsky and Feofan Prokopovich, Samarin summarized it in a few words: Ivan's "mystery lies within his soul, which marvelously mixed vital consciousness of all the shortcomings, evils and vices of that century with impotence and inconstancy of will." Ivan's "terrible contradiction" between his superior intellect and his weak will is the basic characteristic that explains his entire nature.

Aksakov made a more complete evaluation of Ivan, although he began from the same viewpoint as had Samarin. "Lack of will and an unbridled will are one and the same," he said of Ivan and pointed out that "Ivan's ruin" and moral downfall occurred when he "cast off from himself the moral bridle of shame" and became addicted to capriciousness, thereby exposing himself to evil influences. Weakness of will, coupled with the strength of a sharp intellect, was one of Ivan's basic features. But another trait was just as fundamental to him. "Ivan IV was the very nature of art, come to life," Aksakov said. Ivan's soul was dominated by images and conceptions that attracted him by their beauty and compelled him to love them and to translate them into reality in his own life. Not cold, sober thought but the quest for beauty and lofty artistic meaning dominated Ivan and drove him to commit the most savage and meanest of his deeds. Therefore we find in Ivan that "there were many motivations in his soul," and these complicated his spiritual nature.

The attempts by the Slavophile school to develop Karamzin's view and to give it greater integrity marked the beginning of a long line of artistic reproductions of Ivan's character. After the Slavophiles we encounter Kostomarov,[17] who dealt with Ivan more than once in his popular works. Then came Count Aleksei Tolstoi, with his *The Silver Prince* and *The Death of Ivan the Terrible*.[18] The impressions they created became popular. And when Antokolsky, Repin and Vasnetsov[19] embodied this view in precise portraits, everyone began to feel that Ivan had become understandable and obvious, that everything about him could be understood through psychology and pathology. Ivan's extraordinary refinement of cruelty, the fickleness of his moods, his wedding of a sharp intellect to an obviously weak will and his inclination to succumb to outside influences—all these traits attracted pathologists to Ivan. As a result, a sizable medical literature dealing with Ivan was gradually created. N.P. Likhachev has attentively studied and interpreted this literature.[20] To the historian using the scientific critical method all of this literature seems unscientific, its diagnoses capricious and based on facile and completely groundless conjecture. There is no reason to believe these doctors who, three hundred years after the death of their patient and on the basis of unverified hearsay and opinions, diagnose him as "paranoid," "a degenerate psychopath" possessed of "violent mental derangement" (*mania furibunda*) and "delirious notions" and who generally lead us to pronounce Ivan a sick and completely irresponsible individual.

A conclusion of this sort is the natural conclusion of the scientific-literary school which, in studying Ivan's era, restricts its concern to the central figure of that period and seeks in the character of its central figure the key to understanding that historical moment in all its complexity. Men are generally inclined to declare meaningless that which they cannot understand and to consider abnormal whatever strikes them as strange. Cognizant of this human weakness, Kostomarov wrote of Ivan that "he assuredly was not stupid," at a time when his contemporaries were considering Ivan "a man of miraculous intelligence." Although physicians have regarded Ivan a mad degenerate, Ivan's fellow Russians considered him a great political force, even during the last years of his life. A sensible historical method patiently seeks clues to the incomprehensible and explanations of that which is strange; without forming hasty and irrevocable conclusions, it searches for new ways to interpret phenomena that do not yield readily to research.

The Russian public was first exposed to a correct historical method by the representatives of the so-called "historical-juridical" school, led by S.M. Soloviev.[21] Soloviev brought to the study of Ivan's activities his own basic idea that the historical life of the Russian people follows a continuous line of development in which the historical life of the Russian people embodied the entire process of the development of the patriarchal form of life into state forms. Soloviev wished to determine the role played by Ivan in this process. Soloviev saw Ivan as a positive figure who was the bearer of the state "principle" in the life of his people and the opponent of the obsolete "appanage and *veche*" system.[22] Ivan grasped the problems of his times better than did those contemporaries who were more conservative. He forged ahead, while those around him were stifled by old traditions. He had a state program and

sought broad political goals. One need not hide Ivan's
personal weaknesses, shortcomings and vices; but it must
be remembered that these do not constitute his historical
significance. Ivan's domestic reforms and foreign policy
make him a great figure in history. The historian cannot
understand him otherwise.
　　　Soloviev's viewpoint was adopted by his entire school.
An extreme, artificial idealization of Ivan was perpetrated
in an article by Soloviev's contemporary, K.D. Kavelin.[23]   *Kavelin*
Kavelin depicted Ivan as "great," considered him a pre-
cursor of Peter the Great and lamented that Ivan had
been ruined by his environment, which was "dull," "in-
ane," "indifferent and apathetic" and devoid of "any
spiritual concern." In his fruitless struggle against this
environment Ivan perverted his "grand designs," while he
declined in his personal morals because of his fatal failure
to change this environment.
　　　Kavelin's hyperboles, of course, were not accepted by
the entire historical-juridical school, but the notion that
Ivan could be compared to Peter the Great was developed
further. In his detailed article, "Some Comments on the
Poetic Representations of the Character of Ivan the Terrible," K.N. Bestuzhev-Riumin[24] resolutely promoted this
comparison and drew a parallel between "our two great historical characters: Peter the Great and Ivan Vasilievich the
Terrible." According to Bestuzhev-Riumin's view, they were
"two men of identical character, identical goals and almost
identical ways of achieving those goals." The main difference between them was that one succeeded in realizing his
aspirations, while the other failed. Bestuzhev also saw a
parallel between their respective foreign policies, and especially compared their striving for the Baltic Sea. Bestuzhev, like other historians of this school, paid scant attention to Ivan's personal characteristics and vices. These

Ivan's person shouldn't dom in

traits should be mentioned but should not be allowed to determine the portrayal of an epoch of history or the evaluation of the central figure of that age.

Thus by the 1880s there were two schools of thought concerning Ivan and two ways of evaluating him. The subsequent development of historiography has not abolished either school of thought but has obviously exalted the one that neglected the personal characterization of Ivan and strove to evaluate him as a statesman and as a political force. The scientific method employed by the historical-juridical school exercised a powerful influence upon the development of the science of Russian history. Works by Russian historians began to grow in quality, as well as in volume. For the first time direct use was made of archival materials, especially those dealing with the Muscovite period. During the last decades of the nineteenth century and at the beginning of the twentieth a number of themes dealing with events at the time of Ivan the Terrible were taken up and were developed scientifically. Personal appraisals of Ivan were not allowed to influence the investigation of these themes. Such studies sought to reach an understanding of the governmental mechanism and social structure of Russia in the sixteenth century and to gain a clear appreciation of the domestic crisis which the Great Russian people had recently survived.

This scientific work was successful. The main historical sources of the period were studied—collections of chronicles, cadasters and official material that had survived fires and other catastrophes. The renowned "reforms of local government" [*zemskie reformy*] that took place during the 1550s, it was learned, had been launched gradually, and their mutual connections and consequences were discovered. The financial system of the Muscovite state during the sixteenth century was revealed. The true nature of the oprichnina was determined.[25] The activities of Muscovite authorities in defense of the southern boundaries of the state were studied, as well as the related question of the colonization of the "Wild Field."[26] The composition, structure and way of life of the service class[27] were clarified. Much was explained concerning the process by which the peasantry was bound to the land and by which various categories of slavery developed. The real dimensions of the disorder that affected the populace were clarified, as well as the outcome of that disorder—the depopulation of the center of the state. Moreover, the entire "Baltic Question" was studied, as well as all the peripeties of the international struggle for Livonia and the Finnish coast.

Our knowledge of the historical material of this period became so much more complete and certain that the entire history of the reign of Ivan the Terrible had to be reconstructed. One can only be amazed at the vast difference that appeared, in the span of a single generation, in the treatment of this era in the universities. How little the lecturer of the nineteenth century (or, to be more precise, of the 1870s and 1880s) could offer his audience concerning Ivan the Terrible can be seen in the *History of Russia* of N.K. Bestuzhev-Riumin, who was, in his day, a first-rate professor. How the same material is presented today can be seen by comparing any academic textbook of Russian history, such as V.O. Kliuchevsky's *Course of Russian History*.[28] The enrichment of this era by new and valuable material cannot help but affect our understanding of Ivan himself, his personal role and his personal capabilities.

There is no longer the slightest doubt that Ivan, who received his education and developed his intellectual interests in the company of the Metropolitan Macarius,[29] was one of the best educated men of his age. Nor can there be any doubt that the reforms of the 1550s were a complete

system of measures that encompassed many sides of Muscovite life: local administration, including diversification of
the forms of self-government and regulation of the service
class and of service tenure landholding;[30] the organization
of taxation, along with better maintenance of the service
people and improvement of the service they rendered; military organization; ecclesiastical and social concern; the
production of books and much more. Today no one dis-
agrees that Ivan's Livonian War was a well-timed intervention into the international struggle for the right to use the
Baltic sea lanes, which were of paramount importance to
Russia. We no longer hold the old view of the oprichnina,
that it had been the senseless venture of a half-witted tyrant. We now see that it was the application to the great
landed Muscovite aristocracy of the same kind of "removal" that the Muscovite authorities often used against the
ruling classes of lands they had conquered. The removal
of these great landowners from their "patrimonies"[31] was
accompanied by fragmentation of their holdings and reas-
signment of their lands to the conditional use of petty service people. Thus the old nobility were destroyed and a
new social stratum was developed, the *deti boiarskie*,[32] who
were *oprichniki* in the service of the Great Sovereign.

    Moreover, there has come to light an important and
interesting aspect of the work carried on by the Muscovite
government during the most dismal and darkest period of
Ivan's life, the years of his political reverses and domestic
terror. This was the concern of the government to strength-
en the southern border of the state and to settle the "Wild
Field." Under pressure from many sides, Ivan's government
initiated a series of coordinated efforts aimed at defending
its southern frontier and, as always, showed broad initiative,
business-like energy and the ability to coordinate the efforts
of the administration with the assistance rendered by local

authorities. The old notion that the last years of Ivan's life
marked a period of despondent inertia and mindless savagery faded away, as there unfolded before historians the picture of Ivan pursuing his customary wide-ranging activities.
Finally, when the causes and course of the social crisis
that led to the devastation of the center of the Muscovite
state by the 1580s were explained, Ivan personally was cleared of the charge that, because of his alleged cowardice and
worthlessness, he allowed his gifted enemy, Stefan Bathory,
to triumph over him. It happens that the crisis developed
so rapidly that Ivan was deprived of all the resources needed to continue the struggle and that in this instance Ivan
hardly could have exerted personal influence over the course
of events.

In short, every success, however limited, in studying
this era has tended to enhance Ivan's stature as a politician
and a ruler, while the question of his personal traits and
shortcomings has grown less important for a general understanding of his times. Study of Ivan's governmental activity presents the historian with a broad and complex picture
that has the same features for the beginning and the end
of. Ivan's reign. The men around Ivan changed and their
influence upon him may have changed, and Ivan himself
may have lived virtuously or viciously. Yet for all this the
characteristics of Muscovite policy during his reign remained constant. That policy was always broad in its dimensions and was distinguished for its daring initiative, broad
conceptions and energetic implementation of planned measures. Clearly Ivan himself was responsible for these features; they did not originate with Silvester, nor did they
pass away with Basmanov and Maliuta Skuratov.[33] And
Ivan was the same person during the second period of his
reforms, when the oprichnina destroyed the agrarian-class
structure, as he had been during the earlier period, when

he had reformed the Church and local administration. Ivan
was a powerful force in Russian politics.

Everyone who familiarizes himself with the entire body
of new research on the history of the sixteenth century in
Russia gains this same impression. The latest historian of
Ivan the Terrible, Professor R. Yu. Wipper, begins his work
on Ivan with precisely this attitude toward his subject. But
having used everything that recent Russian historiography
has to offer him, Wipper adds something of his own. At
the beginning of his study he presents a general characterization of the sixteenth century as a turning-point in the
eternal struggle between "nomadic Asia" and "the Europeans," a point when the latter began to realize success in
this world-wide struggle. From this universal historical viewpoint Professor Wipper offers an appreciation not only of
Muscovite policy in the sixteenth century but specifically of
Ivan himself. "As part of the new political world of Europe,"
he wrote, "the Muscovite government had to develop military
and administrative skills, as well as dexterity in strategic warfare. Tsar Ivan, his collaborators and his followers continued
to play their difficult role with dignity." In recording the
activity of sixteenth-century Russia against the background
of the general course of political life in Europe and Asia,
Wipper is not chary in his praise of Russian political and
military expertise of this time and regards Ivan a major historical figure. Professor Wipper's book can be called not
only Ivan's apology, but his apotheosis. Even when Ivan
is appraised apart from his own national history and is set
against an international backdrop, Wipper shows that he
was an extremely important figure.

This is the latest word that our historical literature
has to offer concerning Ivan. We can no longer regard
Ivan's character with contempt. But perhaps the scales
have shifted somewhat in the opposite direction; scholars

now face the task of striking an exact balance between the extremes of the subjective evaluations portrayed above.

The present study will not presume to play the role of umpire between these various opinions of Ivan the Terrible. Its objective is to present the "image" of Ivan that was formed in the author's mind during his study of the most significant historical material of the period under discussion. In a brief essay many things must be stated superficially or even passed over in silence. But the author will be gratified if his reader derives from this work a firm appreciation of the great moments of the life and work of Ivan the Terrible, as well as of certain undeniable and verified features of his character and his mind. The author has no pretention of recreating a complete characterization of Ivan or a finished likeness of the man, for he believes it quite impossible to do so.

CHAPTER II

IVAN'S UPBRINGING

1 THE GENERAL CONDITIONS OF THE ERA

Ivan chanced to have lived and worked during one of the most important periods in the life of the Great Russian people. Fate had set that people upon an undulating plain, covered with forests and cut with rivers, uninhabited and readily open to settlement. Settlers freely spread across that plain, much as water spreads over a smooth surface. The course of the colonization carried masses of people from the west and the south to the north and the east,

from the old nests of Russian Slavdom on the Dnepr River
to the Pomorie[1] and the Ural Mountains. On their way north
they were hindered only by the forested wastes known as
"portages"—watersheds between the rivers of the Volga region and those of the Pomorie, where forests and bogs finally overcame the energy of these people. On their way eastward their movement was impeded by alien people residing
in the Tatar Kingdom of Kazan—for the most part Cheremisy[2] on the rivers Unzha and Vetluga, and Mordvinians[3]
on the river Sura. Running from north to south, the lines
of the rivers Vetluga and Sura marked the eastern limit of
Russian colonization that extended from its center at Vladimir-Suzdal, just as the line from Beloozero and Vologda
was its northern limit.

Farther to the north, in the Zavolochie,[4] stretched the
area colonized by Novgorod, which differed in character
from the colonized regions of central Russia. Unlike the
mobile traders and plunderers from Novgorod, the peasants and monks from Vladimir and Suzdal had slowly but
determinedly assimilated "the new land" and had leisurely
extended their operations in farming and the production
of forest products from one settlement to another, abandoning their exhausted "wastelands" to undertake "a new
settlement."

This moment, when the wave of colonization rolled
up to these barriers and the impetuous flood of population was thereby somewhat contained, marked an important turning-point not only in the economic life of the
country but in its political life as well. While the populace had been fluid (to use S.M. Soloviev's phrase), the
political authorities had lacked the power to check these
masses of people and bind them in place or organize them
in keeping with the aims and intentions of the state and
subordinate them to the will of the state.

Appanage princes found that their economic and administrative affairs depended upon a migratory populace. An increase of "newcomers" into their lands strengthened and enriched these princes; but a decrease in population lessened their political importance and made them "lean." The migration of population from the Kliazma River to the Upper Volga that occurred after Batu's massacres[5] weakened Vladimir and Suzdal and strengthened Tver and Moscow. The increase in the population of Galich, on the plateau between the rivers Kostroma and Unzha, allowed the fifteenth-century princes of Galich to stand against Moscow and to sustain a long and stubborn struggle with Moscow for supremacy in eastern Great Russia.

The dependence of princes upon the vagaries of the colonizing movement began to weaken when the migration of people was temporarily brought to a halt at the frontiers of the Pomorie and the Lower Reaches.[6] The natural obstacles of the wild and forested portages and the resistance of the people of Novgorod barred them from the north. War with the Cheremisy barred them from the east. Arable land was largely settled during the fifteenth century and farmers became more densely settled in their peasant communities [*volosti*] than ever before.

Thus the grand princes of Moscow gained a definite opportunity to register their population and began to bind it to one or another form of state obligation. The second half of the fifteenth century and the first half of the sixteenth are noteworthy for these efforts to impose obligations upon the people. The princes of Moscow, after they had taken under their sway all the lands of the Lower Reaches and had overcome Novgorod the Great, hastened to "define" their ownership of both areas. Thousands of service landholders were installed on service tenure land with the rank of *deti boiarskie*. On such estates the peasant population was bound over for the sake of the landholders, while the lands worked by free peasants were made to form tax-paying communes, with mutual guarantees to prevent tax-payers from slipping through the hands of these communes.

At the same time a similar effort to bind "free" servitors to the sovereign was carried on even in the upper layers of society. Not only were boyars deprived of their age-old liberties and rights when they were no longer allowed to "depart" from the Muscovite sovereign to serve another lord. Even princes who had once been sovereign in their appanages lost their rights and liberties when they were subjected to Moscow and "voluntarily petitioned to serve" the Muscovite sovereigns. These princes were increasingly constrained in their right to dispose of their appanages, or "patrimonies," and when rendering service became the equals of the ordinary boyars. Like the boyars, they also lost the right to leave the Muscovite service and to exempt themselves from submission to Moscow.

All of Muscovite life became organized in keeping with the idea of "strengthening" the state. In order to serve this ideal some people were bound to state service, which they rendered from their own land, while others were bound to taxation, which was also wrung from their lands. Some rendered state service from patrimonies (hereditary lands) or from service tenure land (official allotments of land), while others had to pay taxes on their "tilled fields of good, average or poor land," or on their residences in the "urban settlements" [*posady*] or on their shops in the "market."

Ivan the Terrible was born precisely at the time when the new state structure had triumphed, when the independence of appanages had disappeared, when Novgorod and

Pskov had lost the last trace of their peculiar political life, when the Grand Prince of Moscow had really become "the Sovereign of all the sovereigns of the entire Russian land," and when the entire populace of the unified country began to acknowledge that it was "bound" to the state. The successful unification and the binding of the people of the land was at that time the evil of the day, the immediate problem that occupied every mind and agitated emotions and thought. All who grasped the meaning of the process that was unfolding debated its significance. Some welcomed it, while others condemned it, lamenting the ancient liberties that had vanished.

Those who admired and esteemed the arising state created what we might call its ideology by designating the Grand Prince of Moscow the highest political power. They called him "the Tsar of Orthodoxy," the successor to the ecumenical monarchs of Byzantium, while Moscow they named as the successor of Rome, the focus of the entire Christian world. Writers who subscribed to this viewpoint expressed sentiment that was very elated, portentous and triumphant. In addressing the Grand Princes of Moscow they did not shy away from lofty epithets and excessive praise when painting in vivid hues the extraordinary successes Moscow had realized in "gathering" the Russian land and in struggling with foreign enemies.

From his very childhood Ivan must have heard and absorbed these joyous hymns of national exultation. They had been adopted by the ruling circle that surrounded him and that had expanded them into an official theory of the power of Moscow and of the state created by this power.

Much later Ivan came to know another prevalent current of public thought, one that can be termed reactionary and oppositionary. There were some who

suffered because of conditions created by the new state order. They lamented the old times that had passed away
and were angered by the new customs, which they called
"disorders." "Hitherto our Russian land lived in peace
and quiet," they said of the earlier era of Grand Prince
Ivan III. When speaking of the era of Ivan III's son, Vasily III, they added: "When a land changes its customs,
that land will not stand for long. Yet here the Grand
Prince changes our ancient customs. What good can come
of this?" To Ivan, who had been nurtured on concepts
of political optimism, such an attitude was, of course,
alien and dangerous. Everything that his grandmother,
the Grand Princess Sophia,[7] and the Greeks and Italians
who had accompanied her[8] introduced into Moscow—
its court and official life—Ivan had to consider "good,"
and certainly not "disorder." The influx into Moscow
of foreign experts and diplomats who had come for
business with his grandfather and father had been a
natural and unavoidable consequence of the political
growth that was casting the principality of Moscow in
the role of the successor of Constantinople and the most
important power in Eastern Europe. Where in all this
was "disorder"?

This was the spiritual root from which Ivan's intellect grew and his spirit developed. The justification of
absolutism and of national unity, the consciousness of
Moscow's ecumenical role, along with the desire to establish contact with other peoples, were the ideals and aspirations of the age, and they became fundamental to Ivan's
outlook on the world.

But before Ivan could acknowledge and accept these
ideals and aspirations, he had to live through a difficult
childhood as an orphan and suffer the moral decay it inflicted upon him.

2 THE TIME OF THE REGENCY

Grand Prince Ivan Vasilievich, the Terrible, was born on August 25, 1530. His father, Grand Prince Vasily Ivanovich, was over fifty years of age at the time. Because he had no children from his first marriage with Solomonia Saburova, he had, to the great scandal of faithful Muscovites, terminated this marriage in November of 1525 and, to a still greater scandal, on January 21, 1526 married an emigrant princess from Lithuania who was of the family of the Glinsky princes. The uncle of this princess, Elena Vasilievna, was Prince Mikhail Lvovich Glinsky, who had grown up "among the Germans," had been educated in their customs and had served the Duke of Saxony. His military exploits had brought him great glory in Lithuania. But after a quarrel with the Grand Prince of Lithuania, he made his way to Moscow, where he was received with great honor. He also brought his brother, Vasily Lvovich, and Vasily's numerous family to Moscow.

But Prince Mikhail did not fare well in Moscow either. He was arrested on suspicion of wishing to "depart" from Moscow in order to return to Lithuania. While he was imprisoned, however, his niece, the orphaned Princess Elena Vasilievna, came of age and the Grand Prince chose her as his wife. Elena had been brought to Moscow as an infant twenty years before her marriage and had been reared and educated according to Muscovite customs. But nevertheless she had come from a foreign family with a cultural tradition that was not Muscovite. Contemporaries used this circumstance to explain the conduct of the Grand Prince who, contrary to acceptable Muscovite morals and in order to please his young wife, "shaved his beard and began to care for his fine appearance" (as Karamzin put it).[9]

But Grand Prince Vasily's second marriage was not to
have a happy future either. The monarch's first child was
not born until five years after the marriage, a fact that gave
evil tongues an opportunity to conjecture that the son, like
Sviatopolk the Accursed,[10] "had two fathers." When the
Grand Princess subsequently drew close to Prince Ivan Feodorovich Obolensky-Telepnev, the gossip was given credence.
But Grand Prince Vasily harbored no doubts. With lavish
ceremony he baptized his son, Ivan, in the Trinity-St. Sergius Monastery.[11] A year after his birth, on his name day,
"the Feast of the Beheading of St. John the Baptist" (August 29, 1531), Vasily triumphantly erected in a single day,
according to ancient Russian custom,[12] a "simple church"
in the Stary Vagankov section of Moscow (where the Vag-
ankovsky Lane is today). He had "promised" this church
as an offering of thanksgiving for the birth of his son. The
Grand Prince "fulfilled his promise, and he took the matter
into his own royal hands, more so than did those who
worked on it. He began work on the church and completed it all in one day. It was also consecrated on that same
day." "Prince Ivan," who was one year old, was the central figure of all these festivities.

Little Ivan, the long-desired "noble branch of the royal root," then became the subject of miraculous tales. It
was said that at the very hour of his birth a violent thun-
derstorm had suddenly erupted, that a certain *yurodivy*[13]
had predicted the infant for whom the Grand Princess had
been longing and that she would give birth to "a Titus of
broad intellect,"[14] that a quarter of a century before Ivan's
birth a monk named Galaktion, from the Ferapontov Monastery, had foretold that Grand Prince Vasily would be unable to capture Kazan, but that his "son, favored with
grace" (and the name "Ivan" means "God's grace") would
take possession of it. Ivan himself read these and similar

stories in the official chronicle collections and from them learned that he was supposed to have a "terrible" temper and a broad intellect and was predestined to become a great conqueror and statesman. But these Muscovite prophets could not foresee the complications and troubles in which Ivan was to spend his childhood and part of his youth.

Ivan lost his father before he was four years old. Vasily died in great suffering; a "sore" on his leg tormented him for two months and caused general blood poisoning.
With a presentiment that the outcome would be fatal, Vasily began to form his council beforehand[15] and gave instructions "on how the land should be organized and the state governed after his death." He was especially concerned with writing a will and spent much time discussing matters with chosen boyars. He seems to have decided to pass the grand princely power on to his little son, Ivan, and to form about him a sort of regency, a boyar council[16] of trustworthy people. These were the regents Vasily chose: the princes Belsky (who were Vasily's second cousins once removed), Prince Mikhail Lvovich Glinsky (his wife's uncle), the princes Shuisky and their kinsman, Prince Boris Ivanovich Gorbaty-Suzdalsky, Mikhail Semenovich Vorontsov, and several others. Apart from this college of executors the Grand Prince entrusted to Prince Mikhail Glinsky, the boyar Mikhail Yurievich Zakharin and his own attendant, the state secretary[17] Shigona, protection of the Grand Princess Elena and guardianship over "how she was to manage without him and how the boyars were to treat her." He also spoke intimately with these people about his desires in general "and gave them orders about everything, how the kingdom was to be managed without him."

The Grand Prince was especially worried and even frightened by his brothers, the appanage princes Yury

Ivanovich and Andrei Ivanovich, who might "seek the realm" entrusted to his son and murder Ivan. When the Grand Prince could no longer conceal his illness from his brothers, he tried to convince them in every way possible that they should remain true to what they had promised and sworn upon the cross, that is, that his son should become sovereign of the realm, that justice should prevail in the land and that there should be no dissension among them. Although they promised Vasily this, his grave doubts were hardly alleviated. Vasily died on December 4, 1533, anxious for his family and for the fate of the state.

Indeed, the Grand Prince had hardly been buried when troubles arose in the government. The appanage Prince Yury was denounced and was arrested by the ruling boyars, with the consent of the Grand Princess. Two months later the second appanage prince, Andrei, was banished to the town of Staritsa in his own appanage and a "statement" of his complete submission to the Muscovite government was extracted from him. Shortly thereafter the Grand Princess Elena, with the cooperation of her favorite, Prince Ivan Feodorovich Obolensky-Telepnev, freed herself from the appointed guardianship and carried out a coup in the government. She arrested her eminent uncle, Mikhail Glinsky, as well as Princes Ivan F. Belsky and Ivan M. Vorotynsky. Another Belsky, named Semen, and Zakharin's kinsman, Ivan Liatsky, escaped the danger of falling into disfavor by fleeing to Lithuania. During this upheaval the Shuisky family was spared[18] and remained in the government, but much power and rule was concentrated in the hands of the favorite, Telepnev, who acted in Elena's name.

The rule of the Grand Princess lasted from the end of 1534 until the beginning of 1538. In 1537 she succeeded in enticing the appanage Prince Andrei to Moscow and

imprisoned him in chains, where he soon died, and also arrested his wife and his son, Vladimir, who were kept under
guard. All this happened at the beginning of 1537. But
only a few months later Elena herself passed away, on April
3, 1538. According to a persistent rumor that made the
rounds at the time, the boyars had removed her with the
help of poison.

Scarcely a week had passed after her death when "on
orders of the boyar council of Prince Vasily Shuisky and
his brother, Prince Ivan, and others who sympathized with
them," Elena's favorite, Telepnev, was seized "and was
consigned to a chamber behind the palace, near the sta-
bles, where he died of hunger and the weight of his chains."
Then Ivan Feodorovich Belsky and Ivan Mikhailovich Shuisky were released from prison. Thus with Telepnev's fall
there was reinstated about Grand Prince Ivan the sort of
regency that had been intended by the dying Vasily. Only
Mikhail Lvovich Glinsky was not part of it; he had died
in prison on September 15, 1536, about two years after
his arrest.

In evaluating the system of government that function-
ed in Moscow during Ivan's infancy and after the death of
his mother, it must be remembered that power resided in
the hands of those families to whom it had been entrusted by Grand Prince Vasily. All of them were intimate
with Vasily's family and were either of his own family (the
Belsky) or of the clan of his wife (the Glinsky) or else were
most noble princes descended from the Rurikids who, having won the sovereign's confidence, inevitably achieved preeminence in the *duma* and the administration (as was the
case with the Shuisky family). Had these magnates of the
palace been able to agree among themselves, they could
have provided an ordinary regency—a dynastic council acting in the interests of the monarch who was their ward.

But they quarreled and caused the period of their rule
to become one of constant discord, from which the sovereign and his subjects suffered alike.
    When we study the several pieces of evidence that
we have concerning this discord, we discover that the enmity among these boyars did not stem from points of principle. The Belsky and Glinsky families always appeared in
the role of relatives of the grand princes and court favorites who lived in complete solidarity with the head of their
"clan." The actions of the Shuisky family always seem
wild and lawless and manifest neither a political program
nor a determining principle. All these clashes among the
boyars therefore appear to have been the result of personal or family animosity, not a struggle between parties or
organized political factions.

    One contemporary has independently discerned the
constant, self-seeking character of these clashes between
the boyars: "There was much hostility among them
based on personal gain and family advancement; each
sought his own interests, and not those of the sovereign
or the land." These most distinguished and influential
dignitaries were patronized by friends and clients who,
using the success of their patrons, began to derive personal benefit and "personal gain" from their advancement.
These clients were given positions of power, in which they
became "as ferocious as lions, while their slaves acted like
wild beasts when dealing with the common people." Neither political pretension nor social aspiration can at all explain the shameful, predatory conduct of these favorites
who seized power over the country during the infancy of
the Grand Prince.
    Ivan had to watch passively when six months after
the death of his mother and the restoration of the regency
of the boyars, the Shuisky family imprisoned Ivan Belsky

and put to death the state secretary, Feodor Mishurin, "for they did not like it that he defended the cause of the Grand Prince." Later, at the beginning of 1539, they forcibly defrocked the Metropolitan of Moscow, Daniel, and forced him into a monastery, "because he was of the same mind as Prince Ivan Belsky." In his place the abbot of the Trinity Monastery, Joasaph, was appointed Metropolitan. But Joasaph proved to have a mind of his own and, when the time was right, in the summer of 1540 insisted upon Belsky's release. This act terminated the dictatorship of the Shuisky family; it was as though the power of the regency had been restored. The invasion of Muscovite borderlands by the Tatars from Kazan during the winter months at the end of 1540 and by Tatars from the Crimea[19] during the summer of 1541 extinguished the quarrels of the boyars and strained every nerve in the Muscovite government toward the defense of the state. But when this danger had passed, the Shuisky family resumed their old ways. Prince Ivan Vasilievich Shuisky spent the entire second half of 1541 in Vladimir with his troops, opposing the Tatars from Kazan. But while there he also planned a revolution, relying upon detachments of troops that were devoted to him. During the night of January 3, 1542 his units burst into Moscow and committed a number of acts of violence. Prince Ivan Belsky was seized and sent to prison in Beloozero, where he was put to death shortly thereafter. Belsky's friends were settled in various towns. The Metropolitan Joasaph fled in terror during the night to the chambers of the Grand Prince, but the boyars, led by Shuisky, discovered him and, in the presence of the sovereign, subjected him to humiliating treatment, dragged him away and exiled him to the Kirillov Monastery. Archbishop Macarius of Novgorod was nominated and appointed Metropolitan in his place.

The Shuisky family again became predominant in Moscow. But the most distinguished member of that family, Prince Ivan Vasilievich, now left the scene, apparently worn out by illness. In his stead the senior line of the Shuisky family came into prominence—the princes Andrei and Ivan Mikhailovich Shuisky and Prince Feodor Ivanovich Skopin-Shuisky. Andrei Shuisky, the grandfather of the future Muscovite Tsar, Vasily Shuisky, became supreme.

A year and a half later a decisive change occurred in the course of the disturbances that beset Russia. In September, 1543 the Shuisky family, in the presence of the sovereign and the Metropolitan, "while in council with the Grand Prince," did violence to Feodor Semenovich Vorontsov, "because the Grand Prince favored and cared for him." He was almost killed and was spared only "on the say of the Sovereign," for Ivan strenuously interceded for him. Nevertheless, Vorontsov and his son were exiled to Kostroma, against the will of the sovereign. While this was happening, boyars insulted Metropolitan Macarius in the court by ripping the robe he was wearing.

The outrage perpetrated against Vorontsov exhausted Ivan's patience. Ivan was now thirteen years old. He detested the Shuisky family for their continuous offenses against him and resolved to seek revenge for their abuses, probably surreptitiously instigated to do so by the boyars. Three or four months after the incident involving Vorontsov, on about January 1, 1544, Ivan suddenly "ordered the kennel keepers to seize the leading member" of the Shuisky family, Prince Andrei Mikhailovich Shuisky. "And the kennel keepers seized and killed him as they were leading him to prison."[20] Those who could not believe that the young sovereign was capable of such conduct said of Prince Andrei that "the kennel keepers killed him near the

Kuretny Gates on orders of the boyars, and he lay naked near the Gates for two hours."

The death of Prince Andrei ended the hour of the Shuisky family. The official Moscow chronicle says that, having murdered this "leading member," the Grand Prince exiled his brother, Prince Feodor Ivanovich Shuisky, and other members of their ruling circle, "and from that time the boyars began to fear and obey the Sovereign." The regency came to an end, for all the principal members appointed to it by Grand Prince Vasily had now departed this life. Mikhail Glinsky was no longer living, nor were Ivan Belsky and Vasily and Ivan Shuisky. Only second-rate or inactive dignitaries remained, such as the princes Dmitry Feodorovich Belsky and Mikhail Yu. Zakharin. These did not master Ivan's will.

Ivan was especially close to his uncles, Yury and Mikhail Glinsky, and their mother (Ivan's grandmother), Princess Anna. The Grand Prince, who was still too immature to govern, now conferred authority upon this family. Cloaked by the young sovereign and seemingly without official standing, the Glinsky family committed many acts of savagery and violence and exerted very deleterious influences upon the sovereign. The years 1544-1546 marked the hour of the Glinsky family, and the nation has preserved unhappy memories of this period. It was said of the Glinsky family that "their slaves assaulted and robbed ordinary taxpayers, and they did not restrain them from doing so."

When Ivan had matured and grown physically strong, he displayed evil tendencies. He tortured animals, "committed excesses," "gathered many young children about himself" and went so far as to attempt to "kill and rob all sorts of people, women as well as men, while impiously galloping and running about everywhere." His "pets" who

surrounded him, that is, the Glinsky family, not only failed to restrain him but even praised him, saying that "this
Tsar will be brave and manly." Taking advantage of his
inclination toward mischief, they "prompted" him to disgrace and execute people. Contemporaries tell us this.
And indeed, during these years Ivan was very quick to exile and execute people, apparently for insignificant faults
and without determining to which boyar circle they belonged. Adherents of the Shuisky faction suffered as much
as did their enemies and opponents.

The fate of Feodor Semenovich Vorontsov is a good
example. We have already seen how in 1543 the sovereign
"favored and cared for" Vorontsov, but the Shuisky family exiled him. After Prince Andrei Shuisky's death, the
sovereign "again drew him close to himself." But in 1546
Feodor Vorontsov was executed along with Prince Ivan
Kubensky, a supporter of the Shuisky clan, because of a
joint denunciation of them both, a denunciation that proved to be false. These were the first steps taken by Ivan
after the official guardianship of the Shuisky family had
been destroyed and the unofficial guardianship of the
Glinsky family had been established.

It is hardly surprising that the bloodshed and robbery in
the upper classes occasioned mutiny and bloodshed among
the lower classes. In 1547, after a series of great fires
in Moscow, mobs of people who had lost all their possessions killed one of the Glinsky family, Prince Yury, then
came "in a rebellious mob to the Sovereign" at the village
of Kolomenskoe and demanded that the sovereign's grandmother, Anna, and Ivan's other uncle, Prince Mikhail, be
handed over to them. But the sovereign did not surrender
them, and they were spared. The property of the Glinsky
family, however, was pillaged and their slaves "perished
without number." "And many unknown *deti boiarskie*

who had come from Severia and were reckoned slaves of
the Glinsky family also perished."[21] Because of this massacre of the hated family, the hour of the Glinskys came
to an end, and with it ended the first period of Ivan's
youth. His life now entered upon a second stage.
     We have dwelt upon these disturbances among the
boyars in some detail, in order to demonstrate exactly
what Ivan witnessed during his childhood. Not an ideological struggle, not great political clashes, but petty hostility and spite, mean intrigues and acts of violence, pillage and caprice—all this he had to observe and tolerate
day in and day out.[22] Against this background Ivan's
first perceptions were formed and his spirit developed.
And everything of a better nature that influenced him
was debased by the unhealthy instincts that had been
aroused by his surroundings.
          Yet something of a better nature assuredly did af-
fect him. Better influences did enter the palace, for example, in the person of Metropolitan Macarius. Macarius came to Moscow from Novgorod with the halo of
literary fame. While archbishop of Novgorod he had
achieved extraordinary popularity and had been considered a "learned" and a "holy" man. He had "told the
people so many tales" with such clarity that all "felt that
God had granted him the wisdom to read Holy Scripture
and to interpret everything with simplicity." When he appeared in Novgorod "the people found great happiness not
only in Novgorod the Great but also in Pskov and everywhere. And grain was cheap, and the burden of taxation
upon monasteries lessened, and slaves had someone to intercede for them, while orphans had someone to feed them."
     These virtues of the pastor were obvious to all, but
Macarius applied them to an undertaking difficult for the
crowd to understand. He resolved to gather into one

collection "all the reading books that could be found in the Russian land." The soil of Novgorod was most suitable for such work, for Novgorod was the most cultured city of all Russia. Macarius spent ten years at this work. He assembled about himself many men who collected literary material and worked on his editorial staff. Among them were state secretaries such as D.G. Tolmachev, *deti boiarskie* such as V.M. Tuchkov, and churchmen, such as the famous Silvester. The result was that by 1541 the *Cheti Minei*[23] was completed, a vast collection of more than 13,500 large pages of "divine" works: lives of the saints, sermons, books of the Old Testament and the like. The collection contained about 1,300 lives of saints alone.

When he was transferred to the position of Metropolitan in Moscow, Macarius relocated his fellow workers in Moscow and there continued his customary labors, amplifying and improving his material. This work went on around the young sovereign, who was in direct contact with the Metropolitan. The sovereign became conversant with everything that was being read at the time, emulated the literary interests of the Metropolitan, fell under his influence, studied under his direction and became accustomed to appreciating and respecting his moral virtues. Because he was little inclined to join political strife, avoided intrigue and was peaceful and devoted to intellectual life, Macarius remained uncorrupted by the clashes of the boyars and their abuses. To the young sovereign Macarius seemed a man from another world.

The gifted and intelligent Ivan readily and easily imbibed Macarius' lofty outlook on life and assimilated, along with literary knowledge, the nationalistic and political ideals held by those who surrounded the Metropolitan. Ivan's imagination was especially fired by their theory of a single, ecumenical Orthodox state under an autocratic

monarch who would be the "Tsar of Orthodoxy." The
rhetoric of Macarius' school suited Ivan's taste, and reading became his favorite occupation. By the time that he
reached his "maturity," Ivan had become an educated,
"bookish" person, one quite advanced by the standards
of the time. His contemporaries described him as "a man
of wonderful reason and very loquacious, who was content with knowledge gained from lessons in books."
    These circumstances caused the duality in Ivan's na-
ture. Had Macarius' influence totally dominated Ivan, it
would have recreated him. But Macarius' influence had
to contend with the atmosphere of the palace, which was
thoroughly poisoned by arbitrariness, violence and depravity. The Shuisky and Glinsky families had sufficiently en-
sured that Ivan would become acquainted with the nega-
tive aspects of life at that time. By committing acts of
pillage and violence in his sight, they seduced him into
caprice and savagery.
    Few of the chronicle accounts that deal with the
young Ivan are expressive concerning his character. They
speak of his viciousness, idle amusements and even plun-
dering. Local chronicles do not conceal their displeasure
when they describe the journey Ivan made with his younger brother, Yury, to Novgorod and Pskov in the autumn
of 1546. The men of Pskov complained that the Grand
Prince, while in their district, had no concern for business
but "raced about everywhere" (that is, galloped about on
horseback) and "spent little time" in Pskov. Ivan's brother also spent little time in the city, "and did not manage
his patrimony at all." Both of them hurried back to Moscow, "after causing the Christians much destruction and
loss of time." The royal sojourn was regarded a disaster.
    Local chronicles report that during Ivan's stay in Nov-
gorod, at the end of November, 1546, Ivan robbed the

Cathedral of St. Sophia. While visiting the cathedral "he mysteriously learned of an ancient money chest concealed in the wall." Returning at night, Ivan began to "torture the doorkeeper and sexton, in order to learn something about the chest." But "after torturing them greatly," he learned nothing from them. Ivan nevertheless broke open the wall "on the staircase that led up to the ecclesiastical chambers" and found there "a great treasure"—silver bullion—"which he poured out, loaded on carts and sent to Moscow."

Once, during the spring of 1547, when the people of Pskov felt that justice was not being rendered in their city, they sent seventy messengers to Ivan in Moscow "to complain of their *namestnik*,[24] Prince Turuntai-Pronsky. The plaintiffs found the Grand Prince in the little village of Ostrovka in Kolomenskoe, where he customarily went "to amuse himself in the coolness of the evening." The sovereign was displeased that they had disturbed him and "singed the men of Pskov and disgraced them by pouring hot wine over them. He also scorched their beards and hair by burning them with candles and ordered them to lie naked upon the ground."

All this happened during the same months when Ivan, under Macarius' guidance, in solemn and touching speeches addressed the Metropolitan and the boyars and sought their advice concerning "the desire of the Great Sovereign to marry and to seek the blessing to rule the kingdom as Grand Prince." In autumn of 1546 he made his frivolous trip to Novgorod and Pskov. In December of the same year Ivan announced to Macarius and to all the boyars, even those "who were in disfavor, that he wished to marry and to be crowned with a Tsar's crown." In January, 1547 he solemnly accepted the royal title. In February occurred Ivan's marriage to the daughter of the *okol'nichii,*[25] Roman Yurievich Zakharin,[26] and the devout procession on foot by the newlyweds to the Trinity-St. Sergius Monastery. And on about June 1 of that year the plaintiffs from Pskov experienced the new Tsar's mocking favor and kindness.

It is clear that Ivan could easily accommodate lofty words and magnificent and solemn ceremonies to base deeds and licentiousness. His mind accepted noble thoughts and his aspirations were bold, but these did not ennoble his soul or preserve him from moral ruin. They lay on the surface like a beautiful coating but failed to penetrate deeply and become part of the spiritual being of the depraved youth.

CHAPTER III

THE FIRST PERIOD: REFORMS AND THE TATAR QUESTION

1 THE YEAR 1547: FORMATION OF THE CHOSEN COUNCIL

A new period in Ivan's life began with the magnificent ceremonies of his coronation as Tsar and his marriage. The festivities in the palace took place almost at the same time as a series of great fires in Moscow, which were accompanied by a popular mutiny and the massacre of the Glinsky family. During Easter of 1547 the Kitai-gorod[1] burned; a week later the quarters of the city that lay beyond the Yauza River burned down. In June occurred the great fire that occasioned the massacre and achieved historical significance because of its connection with Ivan's moral "regeneration." The entire Kremlin was destroyed by fire, as well as almost all the "taxpaying districts" [*posady*] of Moscow. We might say that the city as a whole suffered, "and every flower garden burned up, as well as all the vegetables and grass in the vegetable gardens." It is estimated that 1,700 men died in these fires. The Tsar departed for the village of Vorobievo, where he remained until the city could revive.

In the places that had burned masses of people sought scapegoats for the misfortunes that had befallen them and found them among the Glinsky family and their servitors. They murdered one of the Glinsky clan and went to the Tsar at Vorobievo, demanding that he surrender others to them. The Tsar answered them with executions, and the movement subsided after claiming many victims.

Fully the half of 1547 was a time of intense experiences for Ivan. It is hardly strange that his contemporaries regarded this precise period as the beginning of an inner change in the young Tsar. In his *History of the Great Prince of Moscow*, Prince A.M. Kurbsky very graphically recounts that after the fire and mutiny God miraculously "stretched out a helping hand and gave the Christian land some respite." At that time "there came" to the Tsar "a certain man, a priest in calling, whose name was Silvester, a newcomer from Novgorod the Great, who rebuked him in God's name through the Holy Scriptures and severely admonished him in the awesome name of God and also told him of miracles and apparitions seemingly sent by God .... And it followed that he healed and cleansed his soul of its leprous sores and set right his depraved mind."

Still more graphically has Karamzin recounted Ivan's "regeneration." Relying on Kurbsky's account, Karamzin interprets the word "newcomer" used by Kurbsky in the sense that Silvester burst suddenly upon the Tsar from

somewhere or other and had been unknown to him previously. When, according to Karamzin, "the young Tsar
was trembling at his palace at Vorobievo and the virtuous
Anastasia (that is, his wife) was praying, there appeared a
striking individual in the robes of an ecclesiastic, whose
name was Silvester and who had come from Novgorod.
He approached Ivan with a pointing, menacing finger, look-
ing like a prophet, and proclaimed to him in an earnest
voice that God's judgment will resound over the head of
the Tsar who is frivolous and given to evil passions . . . .
Having shaken his spirit and his heart, he gained mastery
over the imagination and mind of the youth and worked
a miracle: Ivan was made a new man." But in truth, there
was no miracle, just as Silvester's appearance was not sudden. This was merely what D.P. Golokhvostov has called
"the vivid coloring" of an eloquent historian.

It is well established that Silvester had been in Moscow long before the events of 1547; he probably arrived
there in 1542 in the company of his patron, Metropolitan
Macarius. On the other hand, neither the chronicles nor
any other documents lead us to believe that there was a
drastic change in Ivan after the fire of 1547. Only Kurbsky (and only if he is to be understood in the sense that
Karamzin understood him) depicts a sudden change in the
spirit and conduct of the young Tsar. But it is precisely
because of Kurbsky, when we compare his account with
that of the official chronicle, that one can surmise that
the popular mutiny of 1547 really did occasion an important change—not in the Tsar, however, but in the Muscovite government.

After the mutiny the influence of the Glinsky family
came to an end and their control of events terminated.
The mob killed Yury Glinsky, while his brother, Mikhail
Vasilievich Glinsky, who, in Kurbsky's words, "was the

instigator of all evil," fled from Moscow along with "other servile men who were with him." Yet even when Glinsky hid in his villages at Rzhev, he did not feel safe. With the prominent supporter of the Shuisky circle, Prince Ivan Ivanovich Turuntai-Pronsky, he attempted to flee to Lithuania. They began their flight as soon as the ground was frozen, in November, 1547, but became entangled "in the very close and impassable thickets" of the overgrown frontier of Rzhev and did not achieve their objective. Seeking shelter from pursuers, they themselves went to Moscow, where they were arrested. They attributed their actions to fear, saying that "they undertook this flight out of foolishness, overcome by terror at the murder of Prince Yury Glinsky."

But there was no massacre for them to fear at this time. Moscow had been calm for a long time now. The Tsar was celebrating the marriage of his younger brother, Yury, to the Princess Paletsky. During those very days of November, 1547, the advance guard of the Muscovite troops that had been assembled to conquer Kazan set out from Moscow, and the Tsar himself decided to ride out to his army. In short, life in Moscow was following its customary course. Yet the sovereign's own uncle fled to Lithuania, rather than make merry at the wedding of his youngest nephew. With him fled an important boyar who belonged to the Shuisky faction, that is, to a circle of palace nobility that was quite estranged from, and even hostile to, the Glinsky family and that in no way had been a victim of the popular massacre.

Clearly, it was not fear of rebelling mobs that drove the runaways to Lithuania, but fear of the change in the ruling circle in Moscow. Instead of the compromised and beaten Glinsky family, other trusted persons now surrounded the Tsar. They were of such a disposition that Mikhail Glinsky, the "instigator of all evil," and Turuntai, the *namestnik* of Pskov who had oppressed the people of that town while the Glinsky family had been in power, could expect persecution. They accordingly decided to save themselves by fleeing the deserved punishment.

With his usual rhetoric Kurbsky explained to his reader the manner in which this new ruling group was formed about Ivan. After telling us of how the "newcomer," Silvester, came to Ivan, he continues: "At that time a noble youth named Aleksei Adashev became associated with him (Silvester) for the common good and prosperity. And at that time Aleksei was very much favored by the Tsar and was in agreement with him." Silvester and Adashev together persuaded Ivan of the evil of "those former" rulers "who had been extremely vicious," then had them dismissed or "restrained them by the fear of the living God." To take the place of these dismissed and banished rulers, "those above-mentioned vicious beasts," Adashev and Silvester first "enlisted the assistance"of Metropolitan Macarius, who urged the Tsar to repentance and inner renewal, and secondly gathered about themselves advisers—"men of reason and perfection, of venerable old age . . . and others, who, though of middle age, were also excellent and brave, . . . and these they drew close to him in harmony and friendship, so that without their consent he resolved or planned nothing."

The revolution that took place in the palace is evident. The popular mutiny toppled the guardianship of the Glinsky family. Those who happened to become close to Ivan and who had not been part of the nobility that had ruled earlier took advantage of the spiritual weakness of the Tsar "who was given to evil passions." Through personal friendliness and moral force they established their influence over the Tsar and separated from him all his former guardians and advisers: his uncle, Glinsky, as well as those who supported the Glinsky family. Inspired with a desire for the

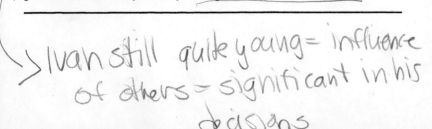
Ivan still quite young = influence of others = significant in his decisions

common good, they took as their objective the moral improvement of Ivan and the betterment of the government.
In Metropolitan Macarius they gained one who could help
and often inspire them.

Thus for the first time a moral atmosphere developed
about Ivan, who hitherto had seen only evil and arbitrariness around himself. The new atmosphere generated a powerful influence not only upon the course of governmental
affairs, but also upon the growth of Ivan's personal aptitude
for governing, with which he unquestionably had been en-
dowed. Yet even now it was impossible to destroy the base
instincts and habits that had been ingrained in him since
childhood.

It is reasonable to assume that the formation of the
new ruling circle about Ivan did not occur at once, but
took place gradually. Adashev and Silvester succeeded in
routing the Glinsky family immediately and in consolidating their influence over the Tsar, who was accustomed to
guardianship and collaboration in matters of government.
But time was required to gather "the men of reason and
perfection" and to organize them into a coordinated and
orchestrated circle. On the basis of the chronicles and
registers of the years 1547-1549 it can be established that
by the autumn of 1547 the Glinsky regime had collapsed;
but indications of the new trend in government policies
are noticeable only at the beginning of 1549. The Tsar
spent all of 1548 in his customary routine: a winter campaign against Kazan without any special result, devout
"processions" to monasteries during the summer, "riding
around" hunting during the autumn "for his royal amuse-
ment," and trips to distant "holy places" in the *Zamoskovie*.[2] Matters of government do not seem to have occupied
Ivan any more than they had previously. It seems that this
is when there gradually came into being behind Ivan's back

the "chosen council" of those who were enlisted as favorites by Silvester and Adashev. A program of action was implemented and relations were established that little by little bound Ivan to complete dependence upon the "council of dogs" (as Ivan himself was later to call the "chosen council").

The composition of this council, unfortunately, is not known exactly. But it is clear that it did not coincide in its personnel with the *duma* "of all the boyars," the traditional council of the sovereign, nor with the intimate *duma*,[3] the intimate dynastic council.[4] It was rather a private circle, set up by the favorites for their own purposes, which they organized around the Tsar not in the form of an institution, but as a gathering of friends "who wished him well." At the head of this circle stood the priest, Silvester, concerning whom testimonials from all quarters agree that he was the all-powerful favorite. The official chronicle says: "This churchman, Silvester, was held in great favor by the Sovereign, who took his advice on spiritual and secular matters. He was, as it were, omnipotent, because all heeded him and no one mocked him or opposed him in any way .... And he wielded great power over all matters, things holy and secular alike, as though he were both Tsar and saint in name and appearance, although he held the position not of saint or Tsar, but of a priest. Yet he did all things only for the best and with his advisers had control of all things." The Tsar himself confessed that, as a child, he had been subject to Silvester's will and wishes, to whom he "submitted without argument."

In Ivan's words, Silvester and Adashev deprived him of all power and so oppressed and persecuted him that "it would have been better to be a slave than to have such power as was mine." The initiative in all this Ivan attributed to Silvester, for it was Silvester who had selected for the "council of dogs" Adashev and others "who pleased him." For his part, Kurbsky also considered Silvester "a blessed man, a true flatterer," who first planned to reeducate the Tsar, then submit him to a guardianship of advisers "of reason and perfection."

Second to Silvester, of course, was the young Aleksei Adashev, who was the same age as Ivan. Perhaps because his duties brought him close to the Tsar (he was Ivan's "chamberlain" and aide [striapchii], that is, he lived with the Tsar), it was Adashev who conveyed to Ivan the influences that emanated from the "chosen council." During the years 1547-1548 Adashev was not a member of the boyar class, nor of the advisory group [dumnye chiny]. He came from the upper strata of the provincial middle service class (from Kostroma) and entered Ivan's court by accident, probably among the "playmates" who were brought into the palace to play with Grand Prince Ivan when he was small. This circumstance later allowed Ivan to say that he did know how "the dog Aleksei" found himself in Ivan's company during the days of his childhood: "It was not our custom to settle batozhniki[5] in our royal palace during our youth." According to Ivan's account, he later favored Adashev—"plucked him from the manure"—because he expected of him "sincere service" and thought that he could replace the "magnates" who were traitorous to the Tsar.

It seems that Adashev's personal traits affected his subsequent career at court. Kurbsky speaks of him with lavish praise, saying that he was "in some ways and in some of his characteristics like the angels" and was so perfect that "coarse and mundane men would find it difficult to believe." When Adashev was with the army in Livonia, Kurbsky claims that not a few Livonian towns were ready to surrender to him "because of his goodness."

Long after Adashev's death, at the beginning of Boris Godunov's career, the Polish archbishop of Gniezno, S. Karnkow-
ski, while in 1585 questioning the Muscovite ambassador,
Lukian Novosiltsov, about Godunov, compared Godunov to
Adashev. He spoke of Adashev in very flattering terms, saying that he was a man who was wise, gracious and efficient
and "ruled the Muscovite state in a manner that Godunov
should emulate." Thus Adashev's personal qualities won
him broad popularity even beyond the borders of his homeland.

Of the other members of the "chosen council" we
know by name (from Ivan's own statements) only Prince
Dmitry Kurliatev, an old servitor of Grand Prince Vasily
Ivanovich, who was granted the title of boyar in 1548 or
1549. Almost certainly the name of Prince Andrei Mikhailovich Kurbsky can be added to the council. About others
we can only guess. But is can be affirmed that, judging
from the general tendencies of the council, the princely
element prevailed in its membership and that princes from
various appanage lineages probably formed a majority.
Ivan himself refers to this in his letters to Kurbsky when
mentioning the chief desires of the members of the council. First of all, in one passage from his letters[6] Ivan sure-
ly means "princes" when he uses the term "traitors" in
saying that traitors intended to pass the throne not to his
son, but to the appanage prince, Vladimir Andreevich. Ivan
felt that Kurbsky was "born of a snake-like fiend," that is,
he was of the princely line, and therefore "breathes forth
venom," that is, betrays the Tsar. "You are evil," the
Tsar says of the appanage princes, "and have inherited your
treason from your ancestors." It is well known that in
1553 the "chosen council" did abandon Ivan, supported
Vladimir Andreevich and did not wish to crown Ivan's
infant son.

Secondly, according to Ivan, as soon as Silvester's influence had become consolidated and the "chosen council" was formed, Silvester "began" to restore the freedom of "landowning by the princes" that had been restricted by the decrees of Grand Prince Ivan III. These had "deprived you (that is, the princes) of your patrimonies," Ivan wrote, "and he (Silvester) granted you the estates you demanded and unfairly distributed these estates like the wind." Translated into our language, this passage meant that the "chosen council" was quick to return to the descendants of the appanage princes the ancestral patrimonies that had been confiscated from them. The council also restored to them the freedom to transfer and bequeath these lands, a freedom that had been destroyed by the Muscovite sovereigns. This act, of course, seemed to be motivated by class interests and revealed the tendency of the council to represent the private interests of the princes. In addition to these definite allusions made by Ivan himself we must consider the general impression conveyed by Ivan in his letters that it was precisely the princes who were the major enemies of the Tsar and hindered his personal freedom and his will. The priest Silvester and Aleksei Adashev were the first non-princes who, together with the princes, attempted to continue the guardianship over Ivan.

In all probability the nature of the relations that sprang up about Ivan can thus be explained. The young sovereign fell under the personal influence of "the priest" and Adashev, who was close to Ivan in age. The two were filled with the desire to improve the government and to select fit people to work in it. They considered the descendants of the appanage princes most suitable for governing the state, for they preserved habits of government and memories of dynastic rule. It was precisely among these people that Silvester and Adashev sought their advisers (apparently

favoring the Riurikovichi to the Gediminovichi).[7] The
"chosen council" that they comprised, standing apart
from customary Muscovite institutions, began to consider, with perfect freedom, a plan for reforms that intended to restore to the state the order that had been shattered during the period of the regency. Implementation
of this plan began during the first months of 1549.

2 THE BEGINNING OF REFORM

On February 27, 1549 the Tsar "in his royal chambers,
before his spiritual father Macarius, the Metropolitan, and
the entire consecrated synod,"[8] delivered to his boyars a
speech of special importance. The chronicler lists several
of the most distinguished of these boyars by name, then
explains that the Tsar's speech was later heard by the entire boyar *duma*. The subject of the speech was abuses
committed by the boyars. The Tsar said that "before I
was old enough to be Tsar, the boyars and their slaves had
inflicted upon the *deti boiarskie* and the peasants great oppression, pillage and injury in matters concerning their
lands, bondmen and other things. But in the future they
and their slaves will cause the *deti boiarskie* and the peasants no such oppression, pillage or injury; and whoever
in the future causes any sort of oppression, pillage or injury will find himself in disfavor and under pain of punishment from me, the Tsar and Grand Prince."
     The *duma* replied to this sweeping accusation with
propriety and dignity. The boyars all begged "that the
Sovereign favor them and not set his heart against them,"
for they wished to serve him and wished him well, just
as they had served his father and grandfather and wished
them well. "And if any of the *deti boiarskie* or the

peasantry should petition the Tsar about anything improper on the part of the boyars or their slaves, and if the Sovereign thinks their complaint justified, let the Sovereign favor them and grant them and their slaves a trial with such *deti boiarskie* and peasants." The Tsar granted them this condition and concluded the discussion with the words: "Henceforth I shall not set my heart against you because of these things. But in the future you must act differently."

On the same day Ivan delivered the same speech to the "generals, princes, *deti boiarskie* and the higher ranking courtiers," that is, to the upper circles of the Muscovite court and administration.[9] On the next day, February 28, the Tsar and the Metropolitan were present when the boyar *duma* passed a resolution closely connected with the Tsar's speeches of the previous day. The Tsar and boyars "decreed that in all the cities of the Muscovite land the *namestniki* were no longer to try the *deti boiarskie* in any instance, except for murder, theft or if they were caught at brigandage. The Tsar also sent his charters[10] to the *deti boiarskie* in all towns."

Ivan spoke of these very same matters to the higher clergy at the Council of the Church, known as the *Stoglav*,[11] at the beginning of 1551: "Last year I humbly asked your forgiveness of my sins, as did my boyars, and you blessed us and forgave us our transgressions. And with your blessing I have also forgiven my boyars all their previous faults and have asked them to be reconciled with all the Christians of my realm for a time, despite past trouble. And so my boyars, chancellery officials and appointed governors of all the land have been reconciled in all things. You also gave me your blessing to correct and confirm the Code of Law [*Sudebnik*][12] as of old, so that justice might be rendered fairly . . . . In accordance with your wish the Code of Law has been corrected . . . and throughout the lands of my realm I have appointed elders, sworn men, *sotskie* and *piatidesiatskie*[13] in every town and in dependent towns,[14] communes,[15] rural administrative districts[16] and among the *deti boiarskie*: and I have signed their charters of local administration.[17] This Code of Law and these charters are now before you. Read them and judge them."

The moral element in all these governmental measures is interesting. When the Tsar launched his reform of local government in 1549, he began his work of renovation by remaking himself. He "spoke humbly of his sins" before the council of churchmen, repented before them with a promise to reform and sought their forgiveness, then called for the reformation and reconciliation of the boyars and other rulers. He repeated this penitential confession before the *Stoglav* Council in 1551 with a very powerful speech, in which he did not spare himself and in which he revealed his own vices, then again summoned his collaborators to moral revival. He set the common good as the objective of his administrative innovations and strove for it not only by preaching repentance and reconciliation but by practical measures as well. He restricted the jurisdiction of *namestniki*, allowed local citizens to participate in their courts, conferred self-government upon local communities, revised the Code of Law and augmented it with a series of resolutions that aimed at allowing justice and fairness to prevail. For the first time the people recognized in their authorities clearly pronounced features of humaneness and concern for the general prosperity.

These were Ivan's first steps toward the reforms that were the glory of his youth. With unusual enthusiasm for moral and practical matters the government carried out changes in local administration and reported them to the Church Council in 1551, asking its approval. These initial

measures were then followed by others, which once again
dealt with local administration and granted local administrative units, in addition to their initial reorganization, the
right of complete self-government. Furthermore, a series
of changes were introduced in the organization and direction of the military forces of the state. The conditions of
service and the way of life of the service class were altered.
Changes were made in the realm of finance and taxation.
It is, of course, impossible to determine the extent to
which the Tsar's own initiative affected all this or how
great was the influence of the "chosen council" upon him.
But there can be no doubt that this strenuous and systematic work by the government was brought to fruition by
Ivan's intellect and was nurtured by his abilities. From an
inexperienced and undisciplined youth Ivan gradually grew
to become an able politician, having passed through a practical school under the leadership of the "chosen council."
But when Ivan matured and his character finally formed,
he not only grasped and mastered the political arts of his
instructors but discovered their class interests. Then the
"chosen council" became, in his eyes, a "council of dogs,"
and he rid himself of its influence and divested himself
of the enthusiasm for morality, which it had communicated to him.

3 REFORMS IN LOCAL ADMINISTRATION

The gradual successes realized by our historical research
have slowly revealed the entire content and course of the
reforming work carried out by the Muscovite government
during the years 1549-1556. Hence, it is now possible to
provide a brief, general outline of the internal consistency
of this activity. As we have shown, this work began with

measures dealing with local administration. The government desired to eradicate the violence, pillage and dissension in the administrative work carried on by *namestniki* and for this purpose came to rely upon the customary forms of autonomous activity that had existed in Great Russia since olden times.

The lands of every "district" [*uezd*][18] (into which the state was divided at that time) were made up of estates of large and privileged landholders, small service tenure estates [*pomestie*] and the "little patrimonies" [*votchinki*] of the *deti boiarskie*, and the communes of the peasantry. The large patrimonies owned by the clergy, princes and boyars were run in a manner similar to feudalism. Here administration and justice were the concern of the owners, and agents of the central authorities did not bother these estates, nor "did they enter them for any reason." But on the other lands the primitive system known as *kormlenie*[19] was in effect. The sovereign appointed a *namestnik* or rural chief [*volostel'*][20] over these local districts to manage the judiciary and the administration. This official was accompanied to the place of his appointment by his menials and ruled with the help of slaves, who received their compensation from *kormy* and "customs duties."[21] This sort of administration brought with it the right to collect income for the use of the centrally appointed governor, and because of this arbitrariness, illegal extortion and violence flourished.

As long as the appointed governor remained in power, it was impossible to contend with him. But when he "departed from his *kormlenie*," he could be followed to Moscow by plaintiffs who sued him for injuries and losses.[22] The government began to take action in 1549 by demanding a general settlement of all such suits ("it decreed a period of reconciliation in all cases") and resolved to institute a system that would make it impossible for such suits to arise in the future. The government excluded the *deti boiarskie* from the general jurisdiction of appointed governors ("in all the towns of the Muscovite land the *namestniki* are no longer to pass judgment on the *deti boiarskie* in any instance, except for murder, theft or if they are caught at brigandage").

In the peasant communes the government took advantage of the ancient forms by which tax-paying and economic life had been organized. The apportionment and levy of taxes and other obligations that were imposed upon the peasant communes according to a common assessment were left to the taxpayers themselves. In addition, the tax-paying community, which was bound together by mutual guarantees, selected a full staff of communal representatives who managed all matters dealing with the taxes paid and services rendered the government. In order to regulate appointed governors, the government commanded these communes to select "court people" [*sudnye muzhi*] to participate in the judicial process. The government further enacted a general law (as part of the Code of Law of 1550) that appointed governors were not to administer justice without the participation of "court people" and "local clerks" [*zemskie d'iachki*] ("and *namestniki* and appointed governors and their agents were not to pass judgment without the elders and the sworn men.").

But the authorities did not stop at this. They quickly reached the conclusion that it was necessary to replace in general the archaic system of *kormlenie* with other forms of local administration that were more in keeping with the demands of the times. Apparently it was from the various forms of local self-government that had developed into a way of life in the northern half of the state, and had worked successfully, that the Muscovite reformers derived the idea to base local administration exclusively upon the principle of self-government. And so in the autumn of 1552, after the campaign against Kazan and while the Tsar was celebrating his victory over the Tatars, Ivan poured out favors and rewards, "and the Sovereign granted *kormlenie* to all the land." This meant that the Tsar announced his decision to abolish *kormlenie* and to undertake a new system of local administration that was more beneficial and agreeable to the populace.

We must consider this new system. When, at the end of 1552, Ivan was leaving to baptize his newly born son, Dmitry, at the Trinity Monastery as was customary, he ordered the boyars "to have sessions concerning *kormlenie*" during his absence from the *duma*. That is, they were to discuss the consequences of its abolition and the means of creating a new administrative system throughout the districts of the country. But this did not happen at once. The Tsar found that the boyars began this work by favoring their own self-interest and "sought to gain enrichment"; most of all, they desired to extract advantage for themselves and for their own class of appointed governors from the abolition of *kormlenie*. To understand this circumstance, one must remember that the destruction of the old system raised two problems: First, who was to replace the appointed governors at the district level and to whom would their duties be relegated. Secondly, how would those who had had the right of *kormlenie* be compensated for the income that would be lost to them after they lost this right. Ivan was of the opinion that the boyars were especially concerned with the second question. Perhaps one must look here for the reason why resolution of this matter was delayed.

According to the chronicle, this matter was not resolved until 1556. Then appeared "the royal decision concerning *kormlenie"*—that the system was to be preserved no longer and that in its stead the communes and districts would elect their authorities from among the local populace. In addition, the Tsar explained that in the towns and districts that adopted self-government, over and above the customary taxes, "there would be established a tax on their businesses and on their lands, and this tax would be collected for the Tsar's treasury by his state secretary." Thereafter, instead of the expenses incurred by the populace for the maintenance of appointed governors, there was instituted a tax ("a *kormlenie* redemption") for the state treasury. From this new source of revenue the Tsar acquired the resources to compensate the local officials who had lost their *kormy* and their "customs duties." Concerning this the chronicle reports that the sovereign "regulated the *kormlenie* of the boyars and the magnates and all warriors with just payments," that is, an annual salary in money for some, and for others "a salary in money every four years, and every three years for still others." Thus the law resolved the problem of local administration.

In practice this resolution was implemented as follows. The populace of one or another locality was allowed to petition the Tsar to recall the *namestnik* or rural chief [*volostel'*] who had been supported by *kormlenie* and to allow the transition to one or another form of self-government. A petition of this sort was followed by a decree from the sovereign addressed to the elected elder who had formerly been attached to the appointed governor: "When this charter of ours reaches you, then you should order *namestnik* (so-and-so) to leave our service (in such-and-such a locality) and should no longer support him as *namestnik* with any salary (from such-and-such a date) or give such salaries to him or to his slaves; rather you yourself shall manage all the monies and other dues which were formerly paid to the appointed governor . . . . And you are to pass judgment on people in all cases. And you (the elder) are to collect revenue from court cases. You are also to select sworn men[23] to collect the income which formerly went to the appointed governor . . . . And when you have collected the receipts of the district, you are to send the money to us in Moscow."

This method was most simple when it was applied to a place where taxation was universal and where the population was homogeneous in class structure. Here the Muscovite authorities relied upon ready-made and ancient forms of self-government in taxation. If the tax-paying commune wished to assume not only financial control as of old, but also the judiciary and the police, which the appointed governor had controlled, then it inherited, practically speaking, total administration of all aspects of provincial life. The agents of this, the most complete form of self-government, were the favorite elders,[24] favorite heads,[25] judges of the land[26] and their sworn men, elders of the court,[27] the good men[28] and other guardians of law and order.

More complicated forms of local self-government were to be found where the same district [*guba*][29] contained both a tax-paying populace and service people, the *deti boiarskie*. In these places the tax-paying communes in the district retained their former features and controlled, through their own provincial elders,[30] economic matters and matters of taxation, while the judicial process and the police, which had been in the hands of the appointed governor, were transferred to a special district elder,[31] who was selected from among the *deti boiarskie*. Then sworn men and a state secretary were chosen to assist him, and these comprised a special office, the district office.[32] Developing from old roots in the land, all these types of self-governing communes preserved local features and at times became very complex in nature.

In essence, Ivan's provincial administrative reform caused to be removed from among the populace an element that was foreign to it—the outside appointed governors and their self-seeking and coarse menials. In turn the reform gave new impetus to the independent work that the populace had carried on from the time of independent appanages and their weak princely courts. The government's interest in the provinces was maintained after the abolition of *kormlenie* by special agents of the central authorities—the town commissioners,[33] the census takers[34] and the census reviewers.[35] All prevailing administrative functions were thus assumed by local organizations, which achieved state-wide importance because of this reform.

4 THE REFORM IN MILITARY SERVICE AND FINANCE

The reform of local administration was closely connected with a reorganization of military service. As soon as the government developed the notion of limiting the authority of appointed governors and abolishing *kormlenie*, another idea necessarily grew in its mind. This was the betterment of the organization and maintenance of the service class, from which the appointed governors had been drawn. From 1550 to 1556 one measure followed another toward the goal of improving the internal organization of the military service class and the service it rendered, regulating the holding of land and improving military technology. Unfortunately, it is impossible to reconstruct the course of the reforming idea in this area of governmental activity. Only isolated measures are known, and these not always in their complete and official form. Some of them survive today only in chronicle accounts that are not always intelligible.

The earliest measure dealing with the service class
was the "decree" of October 3, 1550 concerning the formation of a special detachment of "the better landholding
servitors from among the *deti boiarskie*," one thousand in
number, who were to settle on lands around Moscow.
These "thousand men," who were recorded in a special
"Book of the Thousand," were to be "ready for missions"
of an administrative and diplomatic nature and had to render service in the capital, where they comprised "the regiment of the Tsar and the Grand Prince" (that is, his guard).
The palace staff was recruited from among this "special
thousand," and in the general course of business they were
treated as part of the government, supplying personnel for
command posts in the civil and military administration. All
told, this "thousand" was made up of some 1,078 men who
held service tenure land and patrimonies and formed a middle service class for the capital. They were the apex and
flower of the service class. This was the first measure
adopted.

At the same time and immediately thereafter measures
concerning the military system were enacted. The year
1550 also saw the "the Sovereign's decree" on the restriction of the system of places [*mestnichestvo*][36] during regi-
mental service. In the years that followed, during the military operations against Kazan, a series of measures "on organization in the regiments" was undertaken. The army
was divided into hundreds. The "heads" in charge of these
hundreds were appointed from among the better warriors,
"from the children of great fathers, from fine lads and
from those skilled in military matters." The objective of
all this was the improvement of discipline, and it seems
that this goal was reached. During the campaign against
Kazan in 1552 Ivan observed more than once that the discipline and military spirit of his troops reached a high level.

We can assume that the model for dividing the army into hundreds was the newly formed "chosen *streltsy*"[37] of Moscow—the garrison infantry. In 1550 the *streltsy* in Moscow were organized in six "regiments," each containing 500 men. Each regiment had a commander drawn from the *deti boiarskie*. These regiments were also divided into hundreds with "heads," "with one of the *deti boiarskie* for every hundred men."

In 1556 there followed, simultaneously with the abolition of *kormlenie*, a general decree "to all the people concerning service, and how they are to render service in the future." This decree resulted from "the survey of service tenure land," which was made everywhere, in order to regulate service landholding. After the "census takers" [*pistsy*] and "surveyors" [*mershchiki*] had properly allotted the land to the service landholders, taking away excess land from some and bringing others up to the norm, the Tsar then decreed a general rate of service for all: "For every 135 acres of good, arable land (that is, for 400 acres total in a three-field agricultural system)[38] one man on horseback, in full armor, must be provided, with a second horse for long campaigns." Anyone entitled to hold an estate of more than 400 acres had to provide additional soldiers from among his own peasantry according to the same calculation: one mounted warrior for each 135 acres. But if anyone supplied soldiers over and above the established norm, he was entitled to receive a supplementary "cash grant." This general "code" brought order and regularity to service in the army and made it possible for the government to make an exact calculation of its armed forces.

The government tried to make the same sort of calculation when during those same years it compiled the "Genealogical Directory" [*rodoslovets*] of all the eminent families of the Muscovite nobility and the upper stratum of the

gentry. The authorities also edited an official "Service
Register" [*razriadnaia kniga*], which recorded official
appointments to the most important posts made since
1475. All told, these measures led to the regulation of
service and the equalization of service obligations and
remuneration for service. Thus they encompassed all
aspects of the military organization of the state.

   Directly connected with these military and administrative innovations were the measures adopted in the
realm of finance. We have already observed the resolve
to equalize the service obligations of the *deti boiarskie*
by regulating their holding of land. Ivan himself was
greatly concerned with the idea that it was mandatory
to achieve equality and order in this sphere. Still extant is his memorandum to the *Stoglav* Council, in which
he writes: "I have resolved to send my census takers
throughout the entire land to record and register the
lands that belong to me as Tsar and Grand Prince, as
well as those that belong to the Metropolitan, the pre-
lates of the Church, the monasteries and the Church,
the princes, the boyars, the owners of patrimonial estates and holders of service tenure estates and the lands
that belong to independent peasant communes and all
others, regardless of their owner . . . to determine whose
they are, and to measure land that is arable and not arable, and to measure and record all meadows, forests, all
other resources, so that henceforth there will be no suits
over possession of water and land. Whatever a man has
been given, that he will possess hereafter . . . . And I
shall know who has been granted what, who needs what,
and who renders service on the basis of what resources.
I shall know what is inhabited and what is uninhabited."

   The Tsar's decision to "survey the land" was implemented then and there, in the 1550s. A general inventory

of lands (called a "census" [*pis'mo*]) was begun and two measures were executed on the basis of that survey. First, the status of service landholding by the service people was examined and patrimonial (hereditary) lands were registered. Secondly, important changes were introduced to the method of assessing taxation, and a new unit of taxation was instituted: the *sokha* of 800 to 1,067 acres.[39] Both measures aimed at the just equalization of services, payments and obligations of landholders. It is unnecessary to dwell upon the technical details of this matter. Suffice it to observe that in the realm of agriculture and finance, as in other realms, the activity of the government was distinguished by its broad scope and was motivated by a desire for the common good and for justice.

These activities led to changes not only in the provinces, where the methods of taxation and assessing the burden of taxation were altered, but also at the center of the state, in organs of fiscal administration. Here, parallel with the central fiscal institution of the "Grand Palace" [*bol'shoi dvorets*], which had existed since olden times, other institutions arose, such as the "Great Parish" [*bol'shoi prikhod*] and the Taxation Chancelleries.[40] To further complicate fiscal administration at the center of the state, introduction of the "*kormlenie* redemption" had great effects after the abolition of appointed governors and their *kormlenie*. The taxes from communes that had been submitted to self-government which were based upon the new census were delivered to Moscow in the form of a tax to replace the "income and court dues" of the appointed governor. These taxes were treated as "part of the Tsar's treasury" and were managed by special state secretaries. These state secretaries received the title of Taxation Secretaries [*chetvertnye diaki*], and the chancelleries to which they belonged were called the Taxation Chancelleries. It was from the

Taxation Chancelleries that the service people who had
lost their *kormlenie* received their "just payments" and
were paid salaries in the form of cash. From the name
of the institution, Taxation Chancellery, to which they
were referred to receive their "chancellery money" (*chetvertnye den'gi*), these men were given the name of *chet-
vertniki*.

5 THE ECCLESIASTICAL AND SOCIAL MOVEMENT

If we recall the *Stoglav* Council, then we shall have encompassed all aspects of the reforming work of Ivan and
his "chosen council." Originally called into session to
deal with ecclesiastical matters at the beginning of 1551,
this council acquired broader significance. It became a
state deliberative body, to which the Tsar presented, for
its approval, his Code of Law and the "administrative
charters" [*ustavnye gramoty*] that contained the principles of his provincial reforms. That this was no mere
formality is clear from the Tsar's wording of his questions
to the council concerning provincial affairs. He not only
informed the council of what had already been done but
also asked it to judge and resolve one matter or another.
"Take counsel together on all things and determine how
this matter should be handled in the future. Consult the
administrative charters of your grandfathers and fathers
to see what was decreed." He asked the spiritual fathers
of the council not only for their "benediction" but also
for their signature "on the Code of Law and the administrative charter which will remain in the Treasury," so that
this law would have the sanction of the ecclesiastical authorities as well.

   Ivan was of the opinion that unity of ecclesiastical

and secular authority was generally necessary to the renovating of the state, and he expressed his intention to refer to the council "all our needs and all disorders in the land." Some historians have therefore rightly called the *Stoglav* Council not merely a council of the Church but a council "of the Church and the land." Its program for the development of the Church was just as broad as was the government's program of reforms during those years. As E.E. Golubinsky[41] has put it, at the basis of the council lay "the great idea of renewing the Church through council legislation." To be sure, the council covered all sides of Muscovite ecclesiastical life: Church worship; the administration and courts of diocesan bishops; the way of life of the white clergy;[42] monastery life and monasticism itself; the Christian life of laymen; external piety—all this came up before the council for its judgment. The result of its deliberation was an entire book, the *Stoglav*, which was, in Golubinsky's words, "the code of the council, according to which the administration of the Church was to be executed and Church courts were to function in the future."

These efforts by the government in Moscow elicited thought of a social nature as well. The era of reforms was reflected in the literature of the times through many publicistic works devoted to problems of Muscovite life at that time. These works discussed and condemned the system of *kormlenie*, which "makes towns and communes support magnates, while these magnates grow rich from dishonorable collections from the tears and blood of peasants." The example of the "Sultan Mohammed, Tsar of the Turks,"[43] was pointed out as one who "allowed no one to be the *namestnik* of any city," but "compensated his magnates from his own treasury." In short, the design of the very reform that was actually afoot was here proposed. These literary works discussed means of organizing

the military forces, even while Ivan was adopting his own
measures for regulating and improving the army. They
raised and resolved general questions of administration,
and the Tsar was counseled not to rule through his own
reason alone but with the participation of wise advisers:
"The Tsar should not bear the dignity alone but should
seek the advice of his advisers on every matter." "The
Tsar should be strictly advised on everything by his boyars
and his close friends." At times these works even sounded
the need for the sovereign "to take" broad counsel "con-
tinually," with "all the people, from all his cities every
year." In other words, they expressed the need to con-
voke representatives "of all the land."

Questions of governmental practice were interlaced
with moral themes by these writers, and it is interesting
that the entire body of the literature of the day seems
to exhibit the same sort of moral enthusiasm being expressed by young Ivan himself. Yet it is difficult to determine the extent to which Ivan's reforms were influenced by this literature and the extent to which these
literary themes were a consequence of the governmental
work of the "chosen council" and the Tsar himself. The
chronology of these publicistic works cannot be established with exactness, and their authors are not always
known. It is therefore impossible to substantiate a
causal connection and consistency between the literary
word and the deeds of the government. But in their en-
tirety these works produce a strong impression and depict
the era of Ivan's reforms in extremely vivid colors.

6 THE CONQUEST OF THE TATAR KHANATES

The qualities of the Muscovite government were also expressed in its foreign policy. During the first half of the sixteenth century the problem of the "Tsardom" of Kazan became paramount for Moscow. Founded by the Tatars on the territory of the old Bulgarian kingdom,[44] the state of Kazan was not noted for its internal strength. Here a small number of aristocratic clans, and the *murzy* and *beki*,[45] ruled and quarreled among themselves, keeping Kazan in a state of perpetual civil war. The non-Tatar tribes that formed part of the "Tsardom" of Kazan did not particularly appreciate Tatar rule and easily became estranged from Kazan, yet returned just as easily as subjects of Kazan. The government of Kazan, however, for all its weaknesses, was able to promote the development of trade on the Volga and thus bound to itself the populace of the Volga region. On the other hand, the colonizing drive of the Russian people into the lands of the Cheremisy and the Mordvinians along the Volga forced the Cheremisy and the Mordvinians to seek in Kazan a stronghold against the Russians, and the Tatars were able to render them effective assistance. The Tatars converted this defensive war into an offensive conflict and attacked the Russian frontier, ravaging dwellings and farmland and leading away prisoners. The war with the Cheremisy "went on without end" in the trans-Volga region. This war not only depressed the economy of the farmers but obstructed the routes of commerce and colonization. Communication between the center of the Muscovite state and the Russian northeast, with Viatka and Perm, could be accomplished only through a detour far to the north. Moscow considered Kazan a dangerous and vexatious enemy. The other Tatar hordes[46] did not border on Muscovy, for they lay beyond the "Wild Field." It was possible to arrange a suitable defense against them. But Kazan was Russia's immediate neighbor and, although Kazan itself was not close to Muscovy, its allied non-Tatar tribes were, and these were ruled by Kazan and joined Kazan in its struggle with Russia out of tribal and religious animosity. These neighbors cost the Russian populace dearly, and it was with good reason that the Russian people sang in their songs that "the city of Kazan is built upon bones, and the stream of Kazan runs with blood."

When at the beginning of the sixteenth century the Muscovite government gained a clear picture of the civil wars in Kazan, it attempted to realize advantage from them. First of all, the Muscovite authorities took every opportunity to prepare an army to campaign against Kazan itself. Russians appeared beneath the walls of Kazan, raided its environs and stormed the city itself. But they were unable to hold their ground for very long beneath Kazan, for they lacked bases of operation and were far from their own frontiers, among a restless and hostile population. In order to establish such a base, Vasily III had founded at the mouth of the Sura River in 1523 the town of Vasil' (Vasil'sursk) and stationed a garrison there. Secondly, the Muscovite government endeavored to form within Kazan itself, among mutually hostile groups at court, a Russian party and with its help establish in Kazan khans who favored Russian interests. This strategy was at times successful, but usually the protégés of Moscow did not remain on the throne, and Moscow merely derived the consolation that its policies had greatly aggravated the troubles in Kazan and decisively weakened the enemy.

By the time Ivan had matured and the "council" had formed around him, the problem of Kazan had become

so urgent that its final solution could no longer be delayed.
Ivan understood this well. Operations against Kazan were
mounted every year from the time when Moscow's protégé,
Khan Shah-Ali (Shig-Alei), was deposed in 1546. Following
their usual custom, Muscovite troops appeared beneath Kazan but turned back after a brief time. In 1550, Ivan, who
was present beneath Kazan as part of the usual campaign,
reached an important decision. Pausing at the mouth of
the Sviaga River on the so-called "Round Mountain" (one
might say in view of Kazan itself), Ivan, on the advice of
Shah-Ali, decided to build on that site a military base "for
dealing with Kazan and in order to make the land of Kazan
smaller." From this moment the systematic conquest of
Kazan began.

In 1551 an extensive plan was proposed. In early
spring the state secretary, Vyrodkov, was sent to the district of Uglich on the Upper Volga to prepare timber for
the fortress of Sviazhsk ("to cut timber for walled fortifications and churches"), then to float this timber down
the Volga, accompanied by generals who protected it, to
the mouth of the Sviaga. Then troops "in boats" assembled before Kazan, that is, forces came by the water route
along the rivers Oka and Volga, and troops "from the
field," that is, forces from the right bank of the Volga and
from Nizhni Novgorod. In addition, detachments from the
Kama River and Viatka were sent against Kazan. Thus Kazan was encircled on all sides and was unable to concentrate
its forces to resist on the Sviaga. In May of 1551 the Muscovite vanguard was already in sight of Kazan and, in a
sudden assault, sacked the suburb of Kazan (that is, the
settlement below the walls of the fortress). Then the main
Muscovite army approached the Sviaga and began to erect
a fortress on Round Mountain. The timber floated down
from the province of Uglich was sufficient only "for half

the mountain." The other half of the town "was built
immediately by the people themselves" on the spot, and
"they completed the town in four weeks." When this
fortress-base was completed, it was filled with supplies of
every sort, military equipment and provisions. With this
the operation came to an end.

The founding of the town of Sviazhsk had important
results. The "mountain people," that is, the Chuvash and
Cheremisy who lived on the right bank of the Volga, observed the successes of the Russians and appeared at Sviazhsk with expressions of submission and a desire to serve
Moscow. To prove their good faith they were sent on a
raid under the walls of Kazan, where the Tatars beat them
back. Then their officers went to Moscow for an audience
with the sovereign, where they were entertained and re-
warded. From this incident involving the "mountain people" Kazan itself learned the importance of Sviazhsk. The
Tatars began negotiations with Muscovite generals and submitted to Moscow's will. They surrendered their two-year
old Khan, Utemish-Girei, and petitioned Ivan to return to
them Shah-Ali, whom they had dethroned. Ivan agreed,
and "the Sovereign granted Shah-Ali to Kazan."

But at this point Moscow decided to partition the
Khanate of Kazan. Shah-Ali was to receive "the entire
meadow side and Arsk; but the entire mountain side to
the town of Sviazhsk the Sovereign, by the grace of God,
brought under his own control on the petition of the inhabitants of this region."[47] This decision pleased neither
Shah-Ali nor the people of Kazan. "Tsar Shah-Ali praised
the action of the Sovereign, but he was not pleased that
the mountain side was to belong to the town of Sviazhsk
and not to him in Kazan." Ambassadors from Kazan told
the boyars that "they must not do this, dividing the land."
But Moscow had its way. Utemish-Girei and his mother,

Suiunbeka, were conveyed to Moscow. All Russian captives were freed from slavery.[48] Shah-Ali was installed in Kazan by the boyars. It seemed that the matter had been finally resolved and that Moscow had triumphed. But new complications quickly arose. Shah-Ali aroused general resentment in Kazan because, to strengthen his authority, he "was crude to the people of Kazan," by putting to death one hundred aristocrats who were hostile to him. But his "crudeness" turned against him, and he realized that he "could not live in Kazan." Moscow advised him to bring a Muscovite garrison into Kazan, but he declined, saying that "I am a Moslem and do not wish to become of your faith." Then Moscow came to the decision to support Shah-Ali no longer but to persuade the people of Kazan to accept, instead of a Khan, an appointed governor to act as *namestnik* and to keep Kazan in submission by military force. This *namestnik* would also hasten the withdrawal from the Khanate of the remaining Russian prisoners, for the Tatars "starve these captives and conceal them in underground prisons." Following negotiations with Shah-Ali and those factions in Kazan that supported Moscow, Ivan sent Aleksei Adashev to Kazan in February of 1552 to remove Shah-Ali and to appoint Prince Semen I. Mikulinsky *namestnik* in his place. But just before Mikulinsky was to arrive in Kazan, the people of Kazan "committed treason," shut up their city and refused to submit to the Muscovite sovereign. Warfare then erupted throughout the entire region. The men of Kazan incited against the Russians not only the inhabitants of the "meadow side" of the Volga but also the "mountain people," so that Sviazhsk came under siege. Moscow faced a difficult campaign. The matter was further complicated when the men of Kazan communicated with other Tatar centers and received from the Nogai Tatars[49] military aid, together

with Khan Yadigar-Mohammed, who was installed in Kazan
to replace Shah-Ali. In addition, they also appealed to the
Crimea for assistance.

Moscow adopted several military measures as early as
spring, 1552. The garrison of Sviazhsk, which was suffering from scurvy, was reinforced. On all routes to Kazan
("along all the crossings" of the rivers Kama, Viatka and
Volga) detachments were stationed, "so that troops could
not enter or leave Kazan." In Moscow itself the mobilization of as many forces as possible was mounted. It was
decided to send one army in boats along the Oka and Volga Rivers to Sviazhsk and a second army overland from
Kolomna to Murom and Sviazhsk. Heavy artillery was
sent by water in advance. Ivan himself intended to march
with his own regiment as part of the army that was advancing overland.[50]

In June, 1552, the overland army began its movement
to Kolomna, though without haste, for the Russians expected a possible attack by the Crimean Tatars on the southern
frontiers of Russia. This expectation was realized. The
Khan of the Crimea reached Tula and besieged the town,
but was quickly repulsed by the detachments sent from
Kolomna. Only when it could be verified that the Crimean
Tatars had retreated to their homeland and that all danger
from the south had passed did the Muscovite army advance
from Kolomna eastward through the steppe to Sviazhsk,
which it reached only in mid-August. Now the true significance of the fortress of Sviazhsk, which was, as Kurbsky
said, "in truth superb," became evident. The army entered
Sviazhsk "as though it were coming into its own homes, after that long and very difficult march." Kurbsky attests
that in Sviazhsk there was everything the heart desired. A
huge supply of provisions had been delivered to the fortress

by water, and even "countless numbers of merchants", appeared with goods of every kind.

The siege of Kazan, which lasted a month and a half, was mounted in earnest from Sviazhsk. The operation had been prepared with foresight; and all the principles of the art of siege warfare, as it was practiced at the time, were applied. The besiegers built trenches that ran up to the city, and in these trenches infantry were positioned with their firearms. The siege artillery operated not only from concealed battery positions but also from a "tower," a moveable wooden turret upon which ten heavy guns and fifty light cannon had been lifted into place. The walls of the fortress were undermined—an undertaking that was new to Muscovite engineering. Russians had first become familiar with the use of mining in 1553, when Lithuanian forces took Starodub with the help of mining. At that time the garrison of Starodub "did not understand the craft of mining, for prior to this mining had not been known in our country." Yet fifteen years later Moscow had its own "miners." Ivan had with him beneath Kazan "a German named Razmysl[51] who was knowledgeable and skilled in destroying cities," and instructed him to direct the mining. Several minings were undertaken at the same time, for the Tsar was in a hurry. He ordered Razmysl "to leave" the lesser minings "to his students, while he himself saw to the most important business," in order to achieve the outcome more rapidly. The outcome was reached on October 2, 1552. After an explosion of the major mining the Russians penetrated the fortress and captured it. The Khanate of Kazan had fallen and Kazan became a Russian town.

Although Ivan was later to reproach his boyars because they "had neglected the administration of Kazan" (for after the capture of Kazan little care was taken to

organize the conquered region), nevertheless Moscow bene-
fitted greatly from the victory it had won. The middle Volga region was firmly bound to Moscow by a series of fortresses established in the non-Russian regions and by energetic colonization of the newly-acquired grain-producing ex-
panses in the Volga region. Two or three decades after the
"taking of Kazan," the city of Kazan and the entire bank
of the Volga as far as Astrakhan had become part of the
Russian nation.

Russian detachments reached Astrakhan while the
Khanate of Kazan was being absorbed and, profiting from
struggles among the Nogai princes, occupied Astrakhan "for
the Sovereign" in 1556. Once they had consolidated their
position in this city "so that they could remain without
fear," Muscovite generals "posted Cossacks and *streltsy*
along the Volga, deprived the Nogai of all freedom and
took away from the people of Astrakhan all their fishing
grounds and fords." Thus Moscow had completely at its
disposal access to the Caspian Sea and to the markets of
Asia.

The brilliance of the victories won over these age-old
enemies, the Tatars, the removal of the constant danger
that the Russian people had faced from the warfare of the
Tatars and Cheremisy, the acquisition of new lands for the
Russian economy and the Volga route for Russian trade—
all this brought Ivan extraordinary glory. All literary works,
from the rhetorical compositions of Muscovite writers to the
unsophisticated songs of the people, glorified the young
Muscovite Tsar as a hero. The people did not hear the private opinions that circulated about the personal cowardice
Ivan had shown during the gravest moments of the general
assault on Kazan, when, in Kurbsky's words, the Tsar's coun-
tenance seemed to change from fear, his heart became

distressed and others had to take his horse by the reigns
to lead the Tsar to the place of battle. Clad in this glory,
Ivan entered the next period of his life and work.

CHAPTER IV

THE PERIOD OF TRANSITION

1 IVAN'S ILLNESS

The Kazan campaign of 1552 and Ivan's grave illness,
which followed in March of 1553, apparently caused a
change in the Tsar's disposition. Ivan had grown to manhood because of the unusual experiences of bloody conflict, the impressions of his journey through an alien region to remote Kazan, and the brilliant political success
that had redounded to his credit. Consciousness of his
own personal predominance in these great enterprises
must have increased Ivan's appreciation of his own worth
and stimulated his self-respect and self-importance. Meanwhile, however, the collaborators and friends who surrounded him—the "council" of the priest, Silvester—continued to
look after the Tsar as regents and guardians. Even during
the days of his greatest triumph over Kazan, Ivan said, he
still suffered the influence exerted over him by his associates. The Tsar had been forced to make the return trip
from Kazan to Moscow in a manner he had not wished.
Ivan said that "I was seated in a boat like a captive, surrounded by a handful of people during the trip through

that Godless and faithless land." In reality, Ivan had sailed
the Volga from Kazan to Nizhni Novgorod, then rode on
horseback from Nizhni. Ivan felt that those who had compelled him to take this route had risked his life by providing him with only a small escort in the unpacified, non-
Russian regions that stretched from Kazan to Vasil'sursk
and Nizhni. With indignation Ivan exclaimed: "They tried
to deliver my soul into foreign hands."

If Ivan had already felt the burden of the guardianship during the campaign against Kazan, then throughout
the celebrations in Moscow that followed this victory the
young Tsar, even in his daze of glory, gratitude and personal triumph, must have become even more sensitive to this
tutelage. He undoubtedly was in precisely such a mood
when he fell seriously ill, and his associates, who were accustomed to guiding the Tsar, came face to face with the
possibility that they might lose him, and with him their
influence. Throughout the critical days when the Tsar's
death was momentarily expected, the worried circle of
Silvester and Adashev showed more concern for their own
future than devotion to the dying Tsar and his family.
Ivan learned and evaluated this fact, and the guardianship
that he had found burdensome now became hated.

The following is what happened during the fatal days
of the Tsar's illness. In keeping with old Russian custom,
the sick Tsar was told directly, albeit with difficulty, that
his situation was critical, and the sovereign's state secretary,
Ivan Mikhailov, "reminded the Sovereign of the need to
make a will." The Tsar then commanded that "his will be
drawn," and herein he bequeathed the kingdom to his son,
Prince Dmitry, who had been born during the Kazan campaign and was still "in the cradle." Aside from Dmitry,
the Tsar's family contained two other princes: the Tsar's
brother, Yury Vasilievich, and his first cousin, Vladimir

Andreevich (who was the son of the appanage prince of
Staritsk who had been ruined by Grand Princess Elena).
According to Muscovite procedure, neither Yury nor Vladimir could succeed the Tsar, for Moscow already adhered
strictly to succession by direct descent. As soon as his
will had been composed, Ivan made his intimate *duma*
kiss the cross "to be loyal to the Tsarevich, Prince Dmitry,"
and the boyars swore the oath with complete willingness
in the sovereign's presence. Only Prince Dmitry I. Kurliatev,
who was reported to be sick, was not present. Kurliatev
was a member of the "chosen council," an accomplice of
Silvester, whom Silvester, Ivan claimed, "had allowed into
the boyar *duma*," that is, made one of the intimate boyars.

The day after the Tsar had "brought his intimate boyars to kiss the cross," the "Sovereign summoned all his
boyars" and personally informed them of his will, asking
them to swear allegiance to Dmitry. Ivan did not wish the
oath taken in his presence, for he was "exhausted," but in
the presence of his intimate boyars in the "Entry Hall" of
the palace. But now Ivan experienced an unexpected complication. The boyars began to make "great quarrels and
shouts and loud noise" in the presence of the seriously ill
Tsar. They did not wish to "serve the infant" and told the
Tsar that during Dmitry's infancy relatives of the boy's
mother, members of the Zakharin-Yuriev family, would rule,
"and we have already witnessed many misfortunes at the
hands of the boyars prior to your majority." "And we
shall not serve the Zakharin family, Daniel and his brothers." Ivan had to deliver a "severe sermon." He demanded new oaths from some of them. Others were told to
remember that they had already kissed the cross and now
must support his son "and not allow the boyars to kill my
son by any device." To the Zakharins (Daniel Romanovich, the brother of the Tsar's wife, and his first cousin,

Vasily Romanovich) the Tsar said: "And you, Zakharins, what do you fear? Do you expect the boyars to spare you? You will be the first victims of the boyars! Yet you should die for my son and his mother and should not abandon my wife to be abused by the boyars." Finally the Tsar went to the Entry Hall and there, after many squabbles and "mutiny," all swore the oath to Dmitry. Then Ivan commanded that Prince Vladimir Andreevich Staritsky also be summoned to swear the oath in his presence. But it took threats by the sovereign and persuasion by the boyars to make him pledge allegiance to his infant nephew. Prince Vladimir's mother, the Princess Efrosina, also reluctantly consented to affix her son's princely seal to the oath.

When Ivan encountered this unexpected resistance over the question of the crowning of his son, he asked the boyars whether "you do not kiss the cross for my son, Dmitry, because you already have another Sovereign?" Ivan did not have to wait long for an answer. That another "sovereign" was indeed being considered by the boyars immediately became clear. It was not Prince Yury Vasilievich, for he could not be considered because of his lack of intelligence.[1] It was, however, Prince Vladimir Staritsky. Ivan gathered much information on this matter. He became satisfied that Prince Kurliatev had used the excuse of sickness to avoid taking the oath with the other intimate boyars, because he had conducted negotiations with Prince Vladimir "to see if they desired him to rule the state." Ivan further learned that Silvester himself was championing Vladimir and had quarreled with the intimate boyars concerning him. Then Ivan discovered that the intimate boyar who had been his father's servitor, Prince Dmitry F. Paletsky, had pledged his allegiance to Dmitry but was now concluding dealings with Vladimir, as with one who would be Tsar, to the effect that after his coronation Vladimir would not bring

harm to the appanage of the dim-witted Prince Yury Vasilievich, who was related to Paletsky by marriage. Finally,
and before Ivan's very eyes, the father of his favorite, Adashev "began to speak" against the Tsar's family, the Zakharin-
Yurievs, which signified that he did not wish to see Dmitry
crowned.

All this information shocked Ivan. While ill he had
learned things that he could never have learned while
healthy. His friends and associates, even while serving
him, had disliked his family and at this moment of crisis
had all but openly betrayed him. At that difficult moment they had not been ashamed to convey their sentiments to Ivan himself, sentiments which he found far from
pleasant, and impressed upon him the importance enjoyed
within the ruling house by the insignificant appanage prince,
Vladimir. Here was a source of danger to Ivan. "And
thereafter," says the official chronicle, "there was great
enmity between the Sovereign and Prince Vladimir Andreevich, as well as trouble and insurrection among the boyars."

2 THE RIFT BETWEEN THE TSAR AND THE "CHOSEN COUNCIL"

Ivan recovered by May of 1553, but his little son, Dmitry,
who had been the cause of all the strife in the palace,
drowned in June of the same year. All the commotion
that had attended Ivan's will and the oath to Dmitry had
been in vain. But the consequences of that clash proved
to be grave indeed. The struggle had come out into the
open and had greatly intensified the hostility among the
boyars, with the "chosen council" on one side and the intimate boyars and the Tsaritsa's relatives on the other. This
hostility seems to have prompted those persons who thought

themselves in jeopardy in Moscow to go over "to the king" of Lithuania. Boyar Prince Semen Vasilievich Lobanov-Rostovsky headed this venture. His "brothers and nephews" were also part of this conspiracy. An investigation disclosed that Prince Semen had concocted the idea of taking flight during the Tsar's illness and that in 1553 he had entered into secret dealings with the Lithuanian ambassador who was then in Moscow, Stanislas Dowojna, passing on to Dowojna several state secrets. Prince Semen then sent his slave, Bakshei, to Lithuania and also his son, Prince Nikita, to prepare passage to that country for others who participated in this "treason." Prince Semen explained the reason for his uneasiness by saying that "Ivan did not favor all of them, brought dishonor to the great clans and drew close to himself junior people" (that is, those who were not noble). "And we were also disturbed," Prince Semen continued, "when he married and chose a daughter of one of his own boyars, thereby marrying his own slave woman. How could we serve one of our own sisters?" Prince Semen had learned how very great was the danger that he would "serve one of our own sisters" when the sovereign fell ill and the Zakharins could have seized everything after his death.

Thus the boyar treason of 1554 sounded the same theme that had been heard during the terrible days of the sovereign's illness. But now a further reason was offered. Ivan's grandfather had married a Greek princess, his father had married a princess from a "great" clan, but Ivan had "married his own slave woman" from an ordinary family that was not princely. This circumstance, as it happened, had humiliated the "great clans" who now had to serve "the non-noble people" of the Zakharin family and "one of their own sisters." Clearly, the princes considered Ivan's marriage unwise and not in keeping with his, or their, dignity.

The possibility of a regency of the Zakharins over Dmitry
they deemed especially humiliating to all princely families.
    Ivan's personal position between these hostile factions
was not an easy one. Before this hostility was expressed in
the open confrontation of 1553, Ivan could have been una-
ware of it or perhaps did not consciously notice it. Silvester, Adashev and the princes were his government; his family, the Zakharins, and the intimate boyars who sympathized with him formed his intimate circle. Decorous relations
could be maintained between the two. But now a rift had
opened, and Silvester and the princes were tainted by the
name of Prince Vladimir. Ivan could no longer preserve his
former trust in the "chosen council" and may have begun
to fear it. Let us remember that Ivan believed that Silvester and Adashev "did not hesitate to accord their own favorites as much power as they did me." The Tsar felt
that all the organs of authority were held by the council.
    When Ivan and the intimate *duma* sentenced Prince
Semen Lobanov-Rostovsky to exile in Beloozero, the priest
Silvester and his associates, according to Ivan, "began to
hold that dog in high regard, and to render him every assistance, and not only him, but his entire clan." Despite
the punishment inflicted upon this "traitor," afterwards
"all traitors began to realize a time of prosperity, while
from that time onward we suffered great oppression." Correctly or not, Ivan was perfectly sincere in considering himself dependent upon and "oppressed" by those whom he
could no longer trust. This explains why he tolerated the
"council" around him long after his emotional break with
it in 1553. He simply feared it. The "council" continued
to execute its governmental work according to the plan that
had been created at the beginning of the reforms that had
been introduced through its influence.
    It was seemingly not until 1557 that Ivan more or less

freed himself from his feeling of dependence upon Silvester
and his "friends and associates." At almost the same time
the work toward domestic reform terminated (for the program of these reforms was considered complete) and problems of foreign policy came to the fore. The fall of the
Khanate of Kazan aroused the hostile energy of the Crimean Tatars, and during the 1550s Moscow had to make special efforts to defend its southern frontiers. In addition,
complications arose on the western borders with Sweden
and, still more so, with Livonia. While assessing the general
political situation determining the immediate tasks of Muscovite policy, the Tsar abruptly broke with the "council"
and turned his attention to the west at a time when the
"council" was stubbornly oriented toward the south. With
this Ivan's emancipation began.

CHAPTER V

IVAN'S FINAL PERIOD: THE BALTIC QUESTION AND THE OPRICHNINA

1 PROBLEMS OF FOREIGN POLICY: THE CRIMEA AND LIVONIA

It would be impossible to recount at length all the circumstances connected with the great struggle for trade routes
and the shores of the Baltic Sea that took place during the
sixteenth century. Moscow was but one of many partici-
pants in this struggle. Sweden, Denmark, Poland and

Lithuania, Livonia, England and northern Germany were
drawn alike into this commercial and military contest.
Moscow could not avoid participation, for the struggle
took place on its western borders and exploited and oppressed Moscow. Changes in the status of the Baltic area
caused Muscovite trade either to quicken or to come to a
halt, Muscovite harbors either to remain open or to become blocked, communications with western countries
either to be mended or to suffer interruption.

By the middle of the sixteenth century the western
Muscovite border had begun to suffer especially from measures undertaken by Livonia from its feeling of fear of Moscow's growth and development. Livonia had attempted to
keep Russia totally cut off from the West. Influenced by
suggestions offered by Reval, the towns of the Hanseatic
League, with Lübeck at their head, had also begun to adopt
a similar policy and to work against Moscow. Both forces,
the Hanse and the Livonian Order, wished to exploit Muscovite markets and to extract from them the goods they
needed (wax, furs, flax, hemp and hides), giving Moscow
as little as possible in return. They were particularly careful not to provide Moscow with weapons and other military
supplies, nor to allow "civilizers"—military experts, doctors
and specialists—to enter Russia. The story of Hans Schlitte,
one of the intrepid enterprisers of this time, is well known.
Schlitte wished to draw Moscow into the circle of Central
European political interests and to provide Russia with the
men and materiel it needed for participation in the European league against the Turks. But in 1548 the authorities of
the city of Lübeck refused to allow Schlitte or the people
he had recruited to pass into Russia, for Livonia had presented to the Hanse arguments concerning the grave danger
of any cooperation with Russia. We can say that it was
this course of action that caused Moscow to become greatly

dependent upon its western neighbor. Without Livonia's approval Moscow could receive nothing from Europe, nor could it send merchants to Europe or use the Baltic harbors that were nearest at hand. The happiness with which Moscow greeted the English merchants who appeared at the mouths of the Northern Dvina River in 1553 is therefore understandable, as is Ivan's willingness to endow them with commercial privileges.

But the possibility of using the northern route to communicate with Europe did not end Moscow's desire to use the western routes as well. The latter were shorter and more convenient, especially those that led to Riga and Reval. Both these cities lay under the complete control of Livonia. But Livonia was a spectacle of internal disintegration, and Moscow, well familiar with the condition of its neighbor, was sorely tempted to seize this moment to gain access to the sea.

The plight of the Livonian Order was obvious to all. Anarchy held sway in this land, and Livonia was wasting all its vitality in antagonism. At the root of this antagonism lay the ethnic enmity of the native Lithuanian and Finnish populace toward their German conquerors. This trouble was enhanced by the class hatred of the peasantry toward their feudal lords and the hostility of city dwellers toward both these classes. The country was bereft of political solidarity. The Master of the Livonian Order was constantly quarreling with other ecclesiastical authorities, notably the archbishop of Riga. The towns, having attained freedom and autonomy long before, tried to emulate the Hanse and occasionally seized control of political leadership in Livonia. The urban aristocracy desired to obey neither the Order nor the archbishop. Finally, the Reformation had penetrated Livonia and had created religious animosity, destroying the internal unity of the

Livonian Order and introducing dissension and instability into all class organizations. This was the final blow to Livonia, and disintegration had to follow.

Moscow hardly understood all the substance of the "Baltic Question" and all the complexity of relations between the Baltic states. But Moscow, to be sure, well understood its immediate interests and the immediate political situation. Livonia's crisis, its internal unsteadiness and its military weakness were no secret to Muscovite diplomats. They considered the possibility and the opportuneness of intervening in Livonian affairs to acquire the harbors needed for Russian commerce, harbors that had controlled Russian commerce to that time. The objects of Moscow's longing were Narva, then Reval and, if success were had, Gapsal and even Riga.

But Moscow also well understood all the complexity of its own political situation. Muscovy's brilliant success in the East and, after the subjugation of the Tatar khanates, its advance to the Caspian Sea and the markets of the East, had disturbed the peace of the Moslem world, roused the Crimean Tatars and upset the Turks. Moscow could expect an attack from the south and southeast. This danger seemed especially fearful to careful people who knew the power of the Turks and the terror they had inspired in Central Europe. At the same time Moscow could not expect to remain at peace with Lithuania and had to be content with a temporary armistice with this country of from two to six years. Border relations with the Swedes were so intricate that in 1555 they had led to a war that had been waged sluggishly and had ended in 1557 with a peace treaty of forty years that was favorable to Moscow (and it seems that this war offered Moscow proof of Sweden's weakness).

Russian minds concerned with problems of foreign

policy held to one of two "orientations." Some maintained that the main task of the moment was that of consolidating the areas conquered by Moscow and the defense, as aggressively as possible, of the southern frontiers. Others considered that the current task was that of obtaining trade routes to the West and access to the Baltic Sea. The first group considered the Crimean Tatars Moscow's major enemy, with the Turkish Sultan second. The second group considered the moment opportune for an assault against Livonia, which then was unable to secure aid from either Sweden or Lithuania, just having concluded peace treaties with Moscow. The former group must be regarded more cautious politicians than the second, but the latter were undoubtedly more sensitive and more daring. The "council"—Silvester and his friends—belonged to the first group. Ivan sided with the second orientation.

If Silvester's faction had been consistent, it would have limited itself to measures against the Crimean Tatars that were in keeping with the practical situation of the time. Defensive troops would necessarily have been held ready on the borders, scouts would have been sent into the "Wild Field" and at times raids would have been mounted against the Tatars, in order to intimidate them. After the fall of Kazan and Astrakhan the Crimean Tatars had to expect Moscow to attack them also. Measures of this sort actually were undertaken, probably at the insistence of the "council." But the great success that these measures unexpectedly achieved turned more impressionable heads and inspired the "council" with the dream of an immediate conquest of the Crimea. Wise caution was forgotten and circumspect programs of action gave way to dreams of castles in the air.

Thanks to good fortune, the aggressive actions launched against the Crimea during 1555-1560 grew from short raids and reconnaissance patrols to impressive operations. Among these were the raids carried out by Ivan V. Sheremetiev, Diak Rzhevsky, Prince Dmitry Vishnevetsky and others. In 1556 Rzhevsky reached the shores of the Black Sea near Ochakov and stirred up "the entire Crimea" against himself. A year later Vishnevetsky mounted operations in the same area and attempted to build a permanent base for himself on the island of Khortitsa in the Dnepr River (where later the famous "Sech" was located[1]). At the same time the Cossack ataman,[2] Mishka Cherkashenin, raided Tatar villages on the Sea of Azov. Noting the extraordinary success of all these and similar undertakings and taking into account the drought and epidemics that were draining the encampments of the Nogai Tatars during those years, the "chosen council" succumbed to temptation and began to urge Ivan "to advance with the great forces under your command against the Khan of Perekop,[3] for the time is ripe." Apparently such recommendations were made not once, but many times. Kurbsky says of himself and his accomplices: "Again and again we entreated the Tsar and advised him to march in person or to send a great army at that time against the Tatars." But the Tsar, to the great chagrin of the "council," did not heed these words. Rather, he turned his attention to the West.

It is now difficult to know whether "the time was ripe" for Livonia or for the Crimea at that moment. But clearly a campaign with "a great army" against the Crimea would have been extraordinarily difficult, while Livonia was near at hand and was obviously weak. In those days an advance against Perekop across the "Wild Field" would have had to be launched from positions in Tula, for south of Tula extended "the steppe," that is, the uninhabited expanse of what is now the black earth belt. Here the Russians did not have such strong-points as Vasil'sursk and Sviazhsk had earlier provided against Kazan. Active defense of the southern frontiers and their gradually increasing population had proved a feasible and expedient course of action; and as long as Silvester's "council" had followed this course, the "council" had been right. But the fantastic project of moving the enormous Muscovite field army across the "Wild Field" to the Black Sea coast was undoubtedly unfeasible. Such a plan would have been a scandalous violation of the rule that the scope of military operations should be extended only with caution.

Twenty years passed after this plan was proposed before Moscow attained appreciable results in settling and fortifying the "Wild Field." Only then did it extend the frontiers of state settlement from the Tula region approximately to the Bystraia Sosna River. At the beginning of the seventeenth century the first Pretender proposed to begin his campaign against the Tatars and Turks from the Bystraia Sosna, from Elets and Livny.[4] But this campaign, of course, had been the political dream of an adventurer, not the mature plan of an astute statesman. At the end of the seventeenth century Prince V.V. Golitsyn attempted to attack the Crimea from a base still farther to the south but, as we know, with no success.[5] The later and more successful campaigns toward the Black Sea by Peter the Great and Münnich[6] demonstrated as graphically as had Golitsyn's campaigns the great difficulty of the endeavor and served as a painful but useful lesson for later operations.

Ivan was undoubtedly right when he refused to "march in person" against the Crimea with "a great army." Although Kurbsky cursed Ivan's advisers who allegedly diverted the Tsar from a Crimean war, calling them "flatterers" and "his comrades in eating and drinking," nevertheless these flatterers, if the responsibility really was theirs, were in this instance wiser then the "brave and courageous men" who incited Ivan toward a risky, even hopeless, task. "The time was ripe" for Moscow in the West, toward the seacoasts, and Ivan did not squander this opportunity to lay claim to part of the Livonian inheritance that was to become escheat.

Of course, it was not Ivan personally who layed the Livonian question before the Muscovite government. The course of events in Moscow's political relations and the entire panoply of relations with Livonia had invested this issue with immediate importance. After 1554 these relations reached a crisis. Moscow demanded that Livonia become its tributary. Tribute itself was of small importance, nor did this demand for tribute rest upon indisputable legal principles. All understood that Moscow's stated intention was merely a pretext and symbolic. Noting that payment of tribute already had been agreed upon in a treaty of 1503,[7] Moscow interpreted this treaty as an earlier indication of the political subservience, if not of the entire Livonian Federation, then at least of the district of Dorpat. Moscow therefore insisted that Livonia refrain from friendly relations with Poland or other countries. Agreement to pay the tribute would have signified Livonia's recognition of its dependence upon the Tsar; refusal to pay the tribute gave Moscow grounds for intervening in Livonian affairs.

For about three years the Livonians fruitlessly attempted to avoid paying this tribute. During these years Livonia suffered bitter civil dissension and an unfortunate war with Poland. In desperation Livonia concluded with the King of Poland, Sigismund Augustus, an alliance against Moscow in September of 1557. By the end of 1557 the Russian army was already poised on the borders of Livonia. In January, 1558 it entered Livonia, and the King of Poland sent the Livonians no assistance.

Thus began Ivan's famous Livonian War. The strike against the enemy came at an opportune time—immediately after Livonia had become the protectorate of another state, yet before help for the Livonians could arrive from that state. No one in Russia was at all displeased that the war had begun. Even Kurbsky, a member of the "chosen council," writes of the Livonian War and his participation in it with fervor. Ivan alone relates maliciously Silvester's and Adashev's lack of sympathy for this "German" war. "And from that time," Ivan wrote to Kurbsky concerning the beginning of the war, "what great burdens we suffered from the priest, Silvester, from Aleksei (Adashev) and from you . . . ! With what sorrows were we afflicted, all because of the Germans!"

Yet it is difficult to believe that Silvester and Adashev were speaking from political insight and were not simply vexed with a Tsar who had not heeded them. No one in Moscow could then have imagined just how complicated the Livonian affair would become. No one expected all the powers that longed to gain the Livonian inheritance to take a stand against Moscow: Sweden, Denmark and the Polish Commonwealth, with the Holy Roman Emperor and all of Germany after them. Moscow rejoiced at its quick and easy victory, not foreseeing that it would lead to bitter military ordeals and fatal domestic disorder.

2 THE COURSE OF THE LIVONIAN WAR

In its most general outline the course of the Livonian War was as follows. At the start of 1558 Muscovite troops devastated Livonia almost as far as Reval and Riga. In the spring they took Narva and several other fortresses. In July Dorpat (Yuriev) surrendered after a brief siege. The

Livonians resisted feebly, sought peace from the Tsar in
Moscow and begged assistance from the West. Now Livonia's internal disintegration stood revealed. Even at this
moment of deadly peril the country could not achieve
unity. Estland and the island of Oesel turned to Denmark
for protection and help, while the archbishop of Riga
sought help from Poland and the Master of the Livonian
Order turned to Sweden. This paved the way for general
intervention in Livonian affairs and the partition of Livonia.

The Russian onslaught was repeated in 1559. Again
Muscovite detachments appeared before Riga and even
penetrated into Courland. During the spring a Danish em-
bassy empowered to treat Livonian affairs came to Moscow and obtained from Ivan an armistice with Livonia for
half a year ("from May until November"). The Danes announced that Reval was "obeying" the Danish King and
therefore asked that the Tsar not touch that city. Although
he granted the King of Denmark a truce "for a brief period," Ivan challenged his claim to Reval, declaring decisively
that he would keep Reval "in his own name." During this
truce Moscow expected the Master of Livonia to make a
personal appearance in Moscow or else send "his best men"
to "petition concerning their faults" and to conclude a
peace "however the Sovereign would grant it to them."
But the Master did not come, and the Livonians used the
period of truce to find defenders and allies against Moscow.
They sought these allies within the Imperial Diet in Germany and in Sweden, Denmark and Poland—in short, where
they had sought them a year earlier—and in the course of
these searches Livonia finally collapsed. This disintegration
took place during the years 1559-1561, when Estland became subject to Sweden, the island of Oesel came under
the protection of Denmark and the Master surrendered

Livland to the King of Poland. But the Holy Roman Emperor nominally preserved supreme authority over Livland, and the Master himself became Duke of Courland, clearly subordinate to the King of Poland and the Emperor. The secularization of Courland concluded the process by which the medieval Livonian Federation was destroyed, and Ivan now had to be considered one of its heirs. Ivan did in fact own a considerable portion of the escheated inheritance, but no one except the Danes wished to recognize his legal right to anything. A proposal was even made that Moscow transfer to their more legitimate owners everything that Muscovite troops had seized before the truce of 1559 and afterwards during the campaigns of 1560 and 1561 (Marienburg, Fellin). But demands of this sort were not presented to Ivan sternly and directly, for the Livonian lands were immediately seized by all claimants, who at once began to contest each other, ignoring Moscow. Because an immediate war between Denmark and Sweden over Estland seemed certain, these powers could not deal simultaneously with Moscow. Denmark therefore proposed to Ivan an amicable partition within Livonia, and Ivan held such a strong bargaining position in these negotiations that the Danish ambassadors humbly asked in the name of his friend, Frederick, King of Denmark and Norway, that Ivan bequeath to the Kingdom of Denmark its portion "in your patrimony in the Livonian land, my Great Sovereign, Ivan, Tsar of all Russia by the grace of God." The Tsar "because of his petition and request" was gracious to the Danish King and bequeathed him his portion. This happened in 1562.

Eight years later a new agreement was reached between Denmark and Ivan. Both parties, recognizing Ivan's supreme rights over Livonia, transferred the country as a whole, including the towns "now under the Lithuanians and the Swedes," to the ownership of the Danish "Prince," Duke

Magnus. Ivan "made him king over his patrimony, the
land of Livland" and wrote: "We give him his crown from
the hands of the Great Sovereign himself and make him our
tributary vassal." Compromises of this sort reduced the
danger of war between Russia and Denmark over the con-
tested towns and lands but did not achieve accord. Both
sides conducted their own peculiar policies and in the end
escaped a confrontation only because the fortunes of war
deserted them and sided with their common enemies:
Sweden and the Polish Commonwealth.

For much the same reason Sweden did not at once
embark upon an open struggle with Moscow. Sweden was
on the verge of its seven year war (1563-1570) with Denmark, the cause of which, by the way, was ownership of
Estland. The Swedes therefore feared to divide their forces.
Sending their troops to occupy Reval, which was subject to
Sweden, they simultaneously conducted peaceful, though
not very benevolent, negotiations with Moscow. In 1561
the earlier peace treaty between Moscow and Sweden was
even reaffirmed when a new Swedish king, Eric XIV, came
to the throne—"that there should be an armistice with him,
just as there had been with his father." But thereupon the
King of Poland, Sigismund Augustus, who concluded a
treaty with the Livonian authorities in 1559 concerning a
Polish protectorate over Livonia, lost no time in demanding (in January and again in August, 1560) that Ivan end
the war in Livonia and set the date for its cessation at
April 1, 1561. At the same time detachments sent by the
King of Poland appeared in the theater of war and the
Lithuanian hetman,[8] Chodkiewicz, suffered his first defeat
at the hands of Kurbsky. Thus Moscow saw the Livonian
War become a war with the Polish King or "with Lithuania."
Ivan countered this political complication with courage.
He did not abandon Livonia but now carried the war to the

Grand Principality of Lithuania. At the beginning of 1563
he was able to inflict upon the enemy a telling blow. A
large Muscovite army besieged and captured Polotsk, while
forward units of this army appeared before Vilna. The
fall of Polotsk caused a great sensation in the Polish Commonwealth. Despite the great victory won by Hetman
Nicholas Radziwill over the Muscovite army in 1564, Lithuania longed for peace. Lithuania went so far to secure
a long truce that it conceded to Russia the parts of Lithuanian territory it had captured. The opportunity to acquire
Polotsk in the same manner tempted Ivan. But he did not
settle this matter alone. Instead, he summoned on June
28–July 2, 1566 an Assembly of the Land [*zemskii sobor*],
a representative assembly of the higher clergy, the boyars,
the service people and the "*gosti*,[9] merchants and all commercial people" (that is, representatives of the trading and
manufacturing class). This assembly rejected an armistice
on the conditions offered and supported continuation of
the war in the hope of further military successes. The war
did continue, though sluggishly. Military operations were
conducted with varying success and alternated with attempts
at peaceful negotiation. Finally, a truce was concluded in
1570 on the basis of *uti possidetis* (each side retaining what
it had gained by the given date). The duration of this truce
was set at three years.

But the war with the Polish-Lithuanian Commonwealth
resumed not after three years, but seven years later, in 1577.
The interval between 1570 and 1577 was filled with events
that were very important to Russia and to Ivan himself.
First, a serious peril arose from Turkey and the Crimea.
Secondly, a rift occurred with Sweden. Thirdly, there
arose the issue of uniting Moscow and Lithuania (and even
Poland) through the selection of Ivan for the Polish-Lithuanian throne upon the death of King Sigismund Agusutus.

But this matter was settled through a complete rebuff to the Muscovite candidacy. The complexity of political events during these years was extraordinary and was magnified by the grave domestic crisis that arose within the Muscovite state and shattered its power in foreign affairs. The Turks and the Tatars had begun to stage operations against Moscow as early as 1569. In the spring of that year Sultan Selim sent sizeable forces of Turks, Nogais and Crimeans against Astrakhan. They were to proceed from the Sea of Azov to the Volga via the Don River by making "portages," then go downstream to Astrakhan. Conditions of climate and terrain did not permit this plan to succeed. Only their advance guards approached the lower reaches of the Volga, then quickly retreated out of fear of wintering on the steppe within sight of the Russian forces. To compensate for this setback, the Crimean Khan made a successful raid on Moscow in 1571. Ivan had guarded his southern border during the entire summer of 1570 and had not encountered the Khan. But the following year Muscovite traitors showed the Khan a roundabout route that allowed him to reach Moscow without difficulty and burn the city. The Kremlin alone was saved; all other parts of the city perished in the fire. Many people were burned to death, and wares and property were consumed by the flames. The disaster reached immense proportions. Ivan saved himself by fleeing from the Tatar raid to Rostov and was not present during the attempts by the boyars to drive the enemy from Moscow. The Crimeans wished to repeat this attack on Moscow the next year, 1572, but were defeated near the city by Prince Mikhail I. Vorotynsky and were routed. With this rebuff their energy was temporarily exhausted.

During these years the installation of Duke Magnus as "king" of Livonia was completed and Ivan's rift with

Sweden occurred. Supported by Moscow, Magnus initiated
a siege of Reval, and the Muscovite government became
openly hostile in its relations with the Swedes because of
the success of its "vassal." But when Magnus had to re-
treat from Reval after gaining nothing, Ivan himself began
a campaign into Estland in 1572-1573. The Russians captured several fortified castles but generally had little success.
The affair dragged on listlessly for years, and the Swedes
had no objection to signing a peace. "We ourselves cannot
understand," the Swedish King John wrote to Ivan, "why
you are warring on us." If the issue were simply Reval,
the Swedes were prepared to let the Holy Roman Emperor
become the supreme sovereign of the city. "Then you can
derive income from Reval through the Emperor." But Ivan
desired to extract income from more places than Reval. In
1575 he seized Pernov and Gapsal, intending to control all
Estland. Then later, in 1577, he turned his attention to
Livland, where his troops clashed for the first time with the
army of King Stefan Bathory, who supported the Swedes.
Thus began the final period of the Livonian War, which
brought to Ivan total defeat.

During the period of truce between Moscow and the
Polish-Lithuanian Commonwealth that began in 1570, the
last Jagellonian king,[10] Sigismund Augustus, died (in July,
1572) and the Polish-Lithuanian Commonwealth became
an elective monarchy. Among the candidates to the throne
of the Commonwealth was Ivan himself, who was supported
by the Lithuanian pani[11] and part of the Polish gentry. But
Ivan's candidacy soon collapsed, for the Tsar set conditions
that were very convenient for him but unacceptable to the
Poles, especially to the Catholics among them. This is explained by the fact that Ivan did not seriously expect to become the elected and limited monarch of a non-Orthodox
country. As we know, the name of the Muscovite Tsar had

not been mentioned on the electoral field near Warsaw in
1573 when Henri Valois, the Prince of Anjou, was chosen.
But after a brief visit to Poland Henri fled back to his
homeland and the interregnum in Poland began anew.
Even then Ivan's candidacy had little force. Stefan Bathory, the sovereign prince of Transylvania, was elected king.
    Hungarian by birth, a pupil of the University of Padua
who had also visited Germany, Bathory combined innate
intelligence and natural talent with extensive education and
broad worldly experience. These qualities had helped him
to acquire authority in the Polish-Lithuanian Commonwealth and enabled him to gather sufficient forces and
resources for a struggle with Russia. He became king in
the spring of 1576 and at first was totally occupied with
the task of consolidating his position within the state. But
then he turned to the contest with Ivan with uncommon
energy. In 1577 Bathory's troops began to operate in Livland. The year 1578 was devoted to preparations for a
great campaign and to negotiations with Moscow concerning a truce. Moscow was agreeable to a truce of three
years, but Bathory already had prepared for war and had
no desire to avail himself of such an accord. In the summer of 1579, when Ivan was advancing with a large army
for action against the Swedes, Bathory attacked Polotsk
and took the city. In 1580 he made his way to Velikie
Luki and took that town, which was of strategic importance. The capture of Polotsk and Velikie Luki placed
Bathory on the line of communication between Moscow
and Livland, "near the heart of Muscovy," from which
he had easy access to the upper reaches of the Volga and
the center of the Muscovite state.
    But the king was not aiming at Moscow. He directed
his next blow at Pskov during the summer of 1581, cap-
turing the town of Ostrov on the way. But here Bathory's

successes ended. He had recaptured the Lithuanian territory that had been seized by Ivan and had cut off Ivan
from Livland and had subordinated Livland to Poland. In
summary, he had deprived Muscovy of all the fruits of its
earlier victories. But he saw little success on Muscovite
soil. Pskov repulsed all of Bathory's assaults, and the king
had to remain before Pskov throughout the winter. This
inclined Bathory to negotiate for peace. Ivan also desired
peace, "though it was against his will, for he saw that at
this time the Lithuanian King and his many lands was acting in concert with the King of Sweden." Moscow understood that the enterprise was lost, because both of these
enemies had taken the offensive (during these years the
Swedes had captured Gapsal, Narva and the entire seacoast
as far as the Neva River and the town of Karela). Moscow
rapidly lost the internal strength needed for the struggle.

Peace negotiations were opened with Bathory at the
end of 1581 at Iam Zapolsky (near the town of Porkhov)
and resulted in a truce of ten years. This truce was concluded with the provision that all of Livland and all the
towns that Moscow had captured from Lithuania be transferred to Bathory. Acting as mediator during the conclusion of the peace was the Papal envoy, "a priest of the
Roman faith," the Jesuit Antonio Possevino, whose name
was mentioned in the original copies of the peace charters
as the official representative of the Pope. Somewhat later,
in June of 1582, Bathory succeeded in making vanquished
Moscow pledge not to send troops against Estland during
the entire ten-year period of the truce and "not to take"
the towns, whether Russian or Lithuanian, that had been
captured by the Swedes. This provision marked the virtu-
al cessation of hostilities with the Swedes and ultimately
signified Russia's capitulation. The pledge was formalized
by a treaty with the Swedes in August, 1583, signed on

the river Pliusa. This treaty provided for a truce of three
years on the basis of *uti possidetis*.

3 THE OPRICHNINA: ITS AGRARIAN AND CLASS NATURE

Thus Moscow emerged from the long struggle for the Baltic coast defeated and weakened. In our narrative of the
course of the military operations we have referred more
than once to the fact that Ivan's military reversals coincided with a serious domestic crisis in Muscovite life that
undermined—and very rapidly at that—the economic
strength and fighting efficiency of the country. At the
end of Ivan's reign the Muscovite state was no longer what
it had been at the start of the Livonian War. Ivan's first
campaigns against Livonia and his attack on Polotsk star-
tled contemporaries by the number of armed men that
were involved. On the way to Polotsk the Muscovite army
"overflowed" the roads because of its great numbers, and
the Tsar had to take special efforts to keep the masses of
soldiers in marching formation. But when Bathory delivered his blows against Polotsk, Velikie Luki, Ozerishche
and Pskov, Ivan no longer had enough men to relieve those
fortresses or to send into the field against hostile armies.
To use Kurbsky's expression, Ivan and his entire army hid
in the forest "like one who is a prisoner or a fugitive" and
trembled and ran away, even though no one pursued them.
In fact, Moscow did not send field armies against Bathory
but only opposed him with garrisons, while from a distance
Ivan and his "court" merely observed the movements of
the enemy. During the closing years of the war indications
of the obvious exhaustion of resources needed for this struggle were apparent. As early as the beginning of 1580 Ivan
resorted to extraordinary measures concerning the clergy's

rights to own land and privileges and limited them because
the growth of ecclesiastical landowning "was bringing great
impoverishment upon the military men." Later we shall
see other signs of the economic crisis that befell the Muscovite state. But on the whole, Bathory was beating an
enemy who was already exhausted, an enemy whom he
had not toppled, but who had lost his strength even before
the contest had begun.

The internal disorder in Muscovite life at that time,
with the exception of certain incidental natural disasters,
had two causes. One was Ivan's so-called oprichnina and
its consequences. The other was the spontaneous behavior
of the Muscovite laboring masses who were set in motion
and, foresaking their traditional abodes, began to scatter
from the center of the state to its outlying regions. Both
these reasons were related, took effect simultaneously and
together quickly brought the Muscovite state to domestic
catastrophe. Let us now turn to an explanation of this
complicated process.

The meaning of the oprichnina has been completely
explained through historical research conducted in recent
decades. Russians of Ivan's day failed to comprehend the
oprichnina, for the authorities offered the people no explanation of the measures they adopted; and the measures
themselves seemed very strange. The humble state secretary, Ivan Timofeev, "a reader of books and a writer of
chronicles," says in his "Annals" that the matter was such
that the Tsar "came to hate the towns of his land" and
angrily divided them, "in order to create a schism, as it
were." Another contemporary expressed himself more
forthrightly and said that, upon dividing the state, the Tsar
took part of it for himself and gave the other part to Grand
Prince Simeon Bekbulatovich, commanding that in Bekbulatovich's portion "part of the people should be ravaged and

put to death." Thus it was clear only that there was a
division of the state and that violence was perpetrated
against one of its parts—the zemshchina—while the other
part became the oprichnina. The Tsar's reasons for doing
this were not understood, and it was thought that he was
simply "playing with God's people."

What Ivan did to his peaceful subjects was indeed
strange. Dissatisfied with the aristocracy that surrounded
him, Ivan used against them a measure that Moscow employed against its enemies, that is, "deportation" [vyvod].
In keeping with ancient custom, both Ivan's father and
grandfather, after they had subjugated Novgorod, Pskov,
Riazan, Viatka and other places, had deported the ruling
classes considered dangerous to Moscow and resettled them
in interior Muscovite regions, then sent settlers from native
Muscovite towns to the conquered territory. This was a
tried and trusted method of assimilation by which the Muscovite state organism absorbed alien social elements. This
technique had been applied with special vigor and consistency in the cases of Novgorod the Great and Viatka.
During Ivan's own reign the city of Kazan was remade
into a Russian city after a few years and the Tatar inhabitants of the city were deported to a "Tatar settlement." Deprived of its local ruling class, the conquered territory
promptly acquired a new one from Moscow, then imitated
this class by adopting its orientation toward the center of
the state to which they both owed allegiance.

Because this tactic had known such great success
against foreign enemies, Ivan planned to employ it against
domestic enemies, that is, against those who struck him as
hostile and dangerous. Ivan decided to deport the landowning princes from their hereditary appanage lands to locales distant from their former homes. There they would
have no memories of their appanages nor conditions

conducive to opposition. In place of the evicted aristocracy Ivan settled petty service men, the *deti boiarskie*,
on small plots of service land formed from the old, large
patrimonial estates. The Tsar's implementation of this
plan was accompanied by such a tangle of details that he
bewildered his contemporaries, for they could not grasp
the thrust of his endeavor.

Ivan began his effort by leaving Moscow secretly in
December of 1564. Not until January, 1565 did he send
news of himself from Aleksandrovskaia Sloboda. He threatened to abdicate completely because of the treachery of
the boyars. Only following fervent petitions by the people
of Moscow did he agree to remain in power, but solely
upon the condition that he would not be thwarted "in
imposing his disfavor" upon the traitors "and punishing
them, and taking their moveable property and effects,
and making for myself in my domain a thing apart [*oprichnina*], that is, to make a special court for myself that
could be used completely for my own use." Thus his objective was to oppose "treason," and the oprichnina was
his instrument. Ivan's new "special court" was composed
of boyars and *deti boiarskie*, a new "thousand" who were
selected in the same manner as when in 1550 a thousand
of the best courtiers had been chosen for service in the
capital. This first thousand had been given service tenure
estates in districts near Moscow. Now Ivan granted this
second thousand service tenure estates in the districts of
those towns "that were taken into the oprichnina." These
men became the *oprichniki*, destined to replace disfavored
princes on their appanages.

From the very start the Tsar set aside court villages
and communes for the upkeep of his new court, attaching
to it some of the streets and settlements of the city of
Moscow. He took "into the oprichnina" more than ten

cities and their surrounding districts and transferred from
state coffers to his own accounting the income derived
from other communes and towns, choosing for this purpose large and profitable commercial centers. The original
administrative system of this new "special court," which
was formed in 1565, grew continuously until the very end
of Ivan's reign. The Tsar successively incorporated into
the oprichnina, one after another, the central provinces of
the state, inspected their system of landowning and registered their landowners. He exiled to the frontiers or simply exterminated people objectionable to him and settled
reliable men in their place. Not only were the aristocratic
descendants of appanage princes subject to banishment;
so, too, were ordinary service people, menials and servitors
who were in the company of any lord Ivan found suspicious.

The operation by which landowners were scrutinized
and resettled developed into a massive mobilization of the
service landholding system. Ivan's obvious goal was that
of replacing large patrimonial (hereditary) estates with small
service tenure (conditional) estates. As this process ran its
course, the oprichnina assumed vast proportions. It grew
to encompass the better half of the state, all its central and
northern regions, and left to the old system of administration, the zemshchina, only the outlying districts. The "oprichnina" half of the state had its own government, its own
administration, its own treasury; in short, it was a complete governmental mechanism that worked parallel to and
enjoyed the same rights as the organs of administration in
the zemshchina. As a result, the state really was divided
into two parts, and in 1575 Ivan legalized this partition,
as it were. He appointed as "Grand Prince of All Russia"
the baptized Tatar "Tsar" (that is, Khan), Simeon Bekbulatovich, and placed under his jurisdiction "the land," that is,

the zemshchina. Ivan began to call himself "The Prince
of Moscow" and asked the "Grand Prince" permission "to
examine people, boyars and courtiers and *deti boiarskie*
and court people." During this period, which was admit-
tedly brief (1575-1576), it seemed that the title of Tsar
had utterly disappeared. The oprichnina was called the
"court" of the Prince of Moscow and "the land" became
the "Grand Principality of All Russia."

The direct significance of Ivan's actions is clear. But
we are not at all certain about his motives for instituting
a "special court" to inspect the lands, banish the aristocracy and, finally, embark upon the vicious executions
that attended the activities of the oprichnina. We have
seen that during Ivan's childhood there had been no struggle between boyar parties within the Muscovite court, nor
had there been oppositional factions of boyars or princes.
The hostility expressed by several princely families, though
it darkened Ivan's childhood, was a simple but chronic
difference of opinion among members of the regency to
which Vasily III had entrusted guardianship over the infant
Ivan. The little Grand Prince had not witnessed political
struggle around him, nor had he beheld opposition from
estates or factions. No group of those around him had
aspired to profit by the weakness of the supreme authority by taking into its own hands the government of the
state or by gaining influence over the affairs of state.
From his childhood Ivan had no reason to believe that
his autocratic power was endangered. He must have formed such a belief only in the course of his intimacy with
Silvester and the "council."

We have said that the composition of the "council"
was presumably princely and its leanings, it seems, also
princely. The influence of "the priest" and his "council
of dogs" was very great during the initial years of their

work. Silvester's advisers stifled Ivan's personal will and
imperiously controlled him, seducing him with considerations of the common good, devotion to the public wel-
fare and the notion of service to the state. Ivan obedi-
ently followed his instructors as long as he believed in
them and their ideals. But when, during the days of his
serious illness, he discovered that they were against him
and the family of the Tsaritsa, he trusted them no longer.
He felt that they were pursuing their own objectives, fur-
thering their own policies, that they did not esteem him
personally and disliked his family. In his eyes they were
no longer his dear and faithful servitors but self-seeking
and insincere co-rulers, cunningly depriving him of the
fullness of power and sharing his authority over the state.

Inasmuch as all the machinery of administration was
in their grasp (as Ivan said, "everything was not done" for
the Tsar "according to my will, but according to their desire"), Ivan feared them and their favorite, Prince Vladimir
Andreevich. Seeing that they had already effectively deprived him "of the power vested in me by my forefathers,"
Ivan felt that they could also attempt to deprive him of
this power formally, by crowning Vladimir in his stead.
For the first time, and very keenly at that, Ivan sensed
the danger of opposition around him. He realized, of
course, that this opposition stemmed from class, princely,
concerns and was enhanced by the political memories and
instincts of the princes, "who wished in their treacherous
manner" to become autonomous "sovereigns" equal to the
Muscovite sovereign.

Precisely here must one search for the origins of the
oprichnina. Because he did not dare disperse the "council"
at once, the Tsar tolerated it around him. But inwardly
he became estranged from the "council," and its members
understood that their former relationship had been severed.

The more sensitive among them wished to escape the situation created by the Tsar's distrust of them and his displeasure at their enmity toward the Tsaritsa's family by
fleeing at once to Lithuania. The princes of Rostov did
so, and their act, of course, merely deepened the rift that
was opening. But on the whole the matter dragged on until the beginning of the Livonian War, when the Tsar at
last openly revealed his independence from the "council."
    During the first years of the war, perhaps influenced
by the success that had been won, Ivan finally freed himself from his association with "the priest" and Aleksei
Adashev. Both were dismissed from Moscow—Silvester to
a monastery and Adashev to the war zone. Attempts by
their friends to intercede for them and to gain their return
were refused and tended to annoy Ivan. Their intercessors
subsequently fell into disfavor themselves, yet they made
new attempts to secure the return of the former favorites.
In his reminiscences, Ivan reveals that at first he believed
that, once having become free of Silvester and Adashev,
he could easily abolish the "council." But the friends of
the dismissed stubbornly held their positions, dreaming of
a return to power and in general displaying "an inflexible
mind" on the matter of "making their intentions known
more forcefully" to the Tsar. Then Ivan lost his moral
balance. The matter was complicated by the death at that
time (on August 7, 1560) of Ivan's wife, the Tsaritsa Anastasia, who had long been ill (since November of 1559).
The Tsar linked her death to the "poisonous hatred" that,
to his mind, Silvester and Adashev had felt for the Tsaritsa
and seemed to regard his sad loss the fault of the entire
"council."
    Now Ivan's break with the "council" became a sharp
and violent conflict. With comparative graciousness Ivan
had rejected the first attempts to restore Silvester and

Adashev to favor. "And so at first not one of them suffered the death penalty," Ivan wrote. But now "these
guilty ones received just such a judgment, because of their
guilt," that is, executions followed. Adashev's relatives
were put to death without a trial (Adashev himself died
in Dorpat at the beginning of 1561). These first executions marked a new phase in the development of troubles
in Moscow. They apparently caused general agitation
among the boyars, and this was expressed in their inclination to flee to Lithuania. The Tsar answered the dissatisfaction of the boyars with new repressions. Prince Dmitry
Kurliatev and Prince Mikhail Vorotynsky and their families
were exiled to a monastery in the north. Pledges that they
would not leave Moscow were extracted from some boyars
and guarantors that these pledges would remain unbroken
were demanded of them.

Relations in Moscow became strained not for political
reasons alone. Upon the death of his wife and the removal
of "the priest," Ivan reverted to the habits of his youth
and became dissolute, falling into drunkenness and debauchery. Ivan's overall conduct aroused against him not only
the "council," but all who valued good morals and the fervent "ritual" of palace life. Interesting stories circulated
throughout Moscow of how some of the old magnates condemned Ivan for his sins. Prince Mikhail Repnin was supposedly put to death at the Tsar's command for having
sternly censured a clownish masquerade during an orgy in
the palace.

Unfortunately, little reliable and specific information
is preserved concerning the years 1559-1564, which formed
the interval between the period of the "chosen council"
and the beginning of the oprichnina. But there can be no
doubt that with the dismissal of the "council" and the
death of Anastasia a chasm opened between Ivan and the

upper layers of the Muscovite aristocracy. On one side
stood the Tsar and his new retainers, chosen from the middle layers of courtiers. Among them was only one person
with a princely title (Prince Afanasy Viazemsky) and only
one family that was at all high-born (the Basmanov-Plesh-
cheev family). On the other side was the entire high-born
aristocracy, those who had been close to the "chosen council," as well as those who had been remote from it. Silvester's friend, Prince Kurliatev, was a member of this faction,
but so were others who managed to win the Tsar's disfavor
even though they were estranged from the "council" and
even hostile to it. Among these were the Tsar's young uncle, Prince Vasily Mikhailovich Glinsky, and the senior
member of the Belsky family, Prince Ivan Dmitrich Belsky.
The latter belonged to the family that had been part of
Ivan's guardianship, until they were displaced by the "chosen council."

Thus Ivan's inept and crude break with the "chosen
council" led to his blind hatred of large segments of the
aristocracy. Nothing approaching political opposition
could be seen among the aristocrats. They openly censured the Tsar for his immorality and feared his inclination to subject people to disfavor quickly, even decreeing
the death penalty, as had happened to Adashev's family.
But Ivan interpreted the resentment felt by the boyars
in an unexpected manner. Ivan felt that all malcontents
were in league with the "chosen council" and, assuming
that the "council" desired to rob him of his power, he
attributed the same desire to all boyars and especially, it
seems, to the princes. All of Ivan's extensive correspondence with Kurbsky is filled with suspicions of this sort.
In these letters Ivan readily accuses his guardians of belit-
tling the Tsar's power. They had been the old boyars of
his father, as well as his friends, and associates of Silvester

and Adashev, as well as individual boyars. Ivan explained
that this was the reason that they attracted his anger.
    Ivan was in such a frame of mind when Prince Andrei
Kurbsky, a member of the "chosen council" and one of
Ivan's current favorites, deserted his military command at
Dorpat and fled to Lithuania on April 30, 1564. This intimate adviser not only betrayed the Tsar but even sent
Ivan from abroad a reproachful letter filled with venom-
ous reprimands and serious accusations. This letter had
the strongest impression upon Ivan. Ivan was addressed
in language that he had never before heard in Moscow.
He could assume that the thoughts and feelings that Kurbsky flung in his face were also shared by others. Kurbsky
wrote him in the name of all who were persecuted: "Do
not have the wrong impression that we have already perished, even though you have massacred us, despite our inno-
cence, and incarcerated us and driven us off unjustly . . . !
Those whom you have massacred are standing by the throne
of Our Lord, seeking vengeance upon you. Those who have
been incarcerated and banished unjustly wail to God from
our land day and night!"
    Kurbsky's desertion and letter were the final blows
that shattered Ivan's nerves. The Tsar's irritation prompted
him to adopt those extremes that we now term the oprichnina. To Ivan's mind, the source of all evil was the "treacherous lords"—the princes who had organized the "council"—
while the boyars who had sympathized with the princes
were guilty of capriciousness and opposition. The sovereign's wrath must fall upon anyone guilty of any thought
or action against the Tsar. But the princes had to suffer
a particularly terrible punishment. Ivan resolved to destroy the very basis of their claims to social and political
superiority in the country: their hereditary and privileged
tenure of land on appanages where the ancestors of these

princes had once been sovereign. The old "princely" patrimonies, with their vestiges of an independent way of life
and memories of political power, nourished in these princes
the idea that they could become co-rulers "of all Russia"
with the Muscovite sovereign, who was of their own family
and was not even the senior member of their "generation."
Ivan decided to remove the princes from their patrimonies
to new locales, to sever their connections with local communities, thereby undermining their material well-being,
but, above all, to destroy the foundation upon which rested their political pretensions and upon which their social
superiority had been based.

4 THE CONSEQUENCES OF THE OPRICHNINA

We must assume that Ivan set up for himself in the oprichnina a "special court" in order to liberate himself from the
common bonds of kinship and relationship through marriage
that were strong in the old palace. Lodging himself in his
new palaces (one in the Arbat section of Moscow, another
in Aleksandrovskaia Sloboda), the Tsar surrounded himself
with new servitors and boyars whom he found acceptable
and, with the help of a new "thousand" of *oprichniki*, began to pursue his objectives. Province after province he
incorporated into the oprichnina and "sorted out his slaves."
First of all, he destroyed or removed to outlying regions of
Muscovy the large landowners—the princes and boyars. Their
menials either accompanied their lord or were dispersed and
had to find new lords to serve. The large patrimonies were
then divided into small allotments, which became service tenure estates for the *oprichniki*, whose status was that of the
deti boiarskie. After the large landowners, smallholders
were dealt with in turn. They, too, were removed to new

localities and suffered the loss of their old patrimonies and service tenure estates, and were replaced by new people who, from the viewpoint of the oprichnina, were more trustworthy. In all this the old landowners were, as a rule, sent to the frontiers, where they might be useful in defending the state. The most striking example of this sort of resettlement on the borders was the massive deportation in 1571 of service people from two provinces of Novgorod that had been absorbed into the oprichnina to Sebezh, Ozerishche and Usviat on the Lithuanian border, where they had to begin their economic life anew while guarding the border against the enemy.

The sorting out of "slaves" that occurred during the oprichnina was accompanied by persecution of all who incurred the disfavor of the sovereign and by outright violence by the *oprichniki* against those whom they could abuse with impunity. In the eyes of the people, the entire operation of inspecting and resettling landowners assumed the nature of a disaster and political terror. The sovereign was not merely content with effecting this transformation; he also raged against those whom he suspected of "treason" (or what today we would call unreliability). With unusual cruelty he executed and tortured without investigation or trial those whom he deemed offensive, exiled their families and ravaged their holdings. His *oprichniki* felt no shame when killing defenseless people "for fun" or robbing and raping them. Ridding himself of the earlier frame of mind impressed upon him by the "council," Ivan grew morally degenerate, wallowed in orgies and debauchery and surrounded himself with reprobates, allowing them everything their licentiousness demanded.

Yet even then the Tsar preserved the qualities that his practical training had bestowed upon him during the

period of his first reforms. He completely guided the
course of the government. He conducted affairs during
the oprichnina confidently and steadfastly, moving directly toward his goal and attaining it. The system of princely landowning was shattered; and the princes were torn
from their ancient nests and scattered throughout the entire land. The most eminent members of this class were
destroyed. Their preeminence within the government
was ended. Choice positions in the boyar *duma* and in
the palace now fell to the aristocracy of the new order—
the sovereign's favorites and the relatives of the Tsar's
wives. The Rurikid and Gediminovich princes retained
their positions only when they were able to win the sovereign's favor by their willingness to serve in the new oprichnina system.

During the last years of his life Ivan was able to cele-
brate his victory over his domestic enemies. No longer
was the Tsar constrained by the "sovereigns and governors" who had oppressed him in his youth. By his own
admission, Ivan acted in accordance with an apostolic injunction: "Some are judged mercifully, others are saved
through fear." Ivan finally became "an autocrat" in reality, for he "himself constructed" his realm. But we can
be sure that he also understood the error into which he
had fallen by launching the oprichnina. Probably he never
doubted that he had chosen an incongruous means to
reach his goal. The objective of the oprichnina, the weak-
ening of the aristocracy, could have been achieved by a
less complex method. Ivan's measures, though they proved
effective, led not only to the destruction of the aristocracy
but also to a number of other effects that Ivan could hardly have desired or expected.

First of all, the method the oprichnina used to examine lands held by princes caused the entire land to be

mobilized for service. But this process was compulsory, alarming and therefore chaotic. The massive confiscation of large patrimonial estates, the movement of masses of service landholders, the secularization of Church lands and the conversion of palace and state lands to private holdings to meet the needs of the oprichnina—all this caused a violent revision of relationships on the land and sowed dissatisfaction and fear. The ruin of the large farms of the persecuted aristocracy was followed by the ruin of the farms of ordinary service people with small land holdings; these were, for political reasons, transported from their lands to other lands, in order to make room for the *oprichniki*. What violence and injury, destruction and loss were connected with this movement! On the old land the established economic order of the service man was destroyed. In his new way of life, most often on the frontier, the service man found it difficult to feel at home and become established in these wastelands without peasants, farm implements, livestock or money (although he usually had not had money even in the past).

Lesser people, those dependent upon the service lords, suffered no less than their masters. According to an old Muscovite custom, not only was the property of a man who fell into disfavor confiscated, but his documents as well, his "charters and title deeds." Such title deeds now lost their validity, and the people in bondage, "the slaves of the disgraced boyar," received their freedom, sometimes with the injunction that they were not to join another household. Condemned to a free but hungry existence, these people became an itinerant element dangerous to the established order. The laboring peasant population of lands that were reorganized likewise suffered from the changes, even if they did not fall victim to the pillage and violence of the *oprichniki*. The peasants on large, rich patrimonial

estates had formed communes, with their own elected officials managing taxation and other matters. But when
these patrimonial estates were divided into small service
tenure allotments, the commune was dissolved and the
peasants were dispersed in individual households under the
control of service landholders. They now found themselves in worse conditions, in a state of bound dependence.
Under rich and privileged proprietors the peasants had pro-
fitted from the advantages of immunity. But under poor
and common landholders they now "drew their burden"
without privileges of any kind. Transfer to a new pro-
prietor was therefore a calamity upon the peasants that
forced them to leave their place and seek "new lands."
     Thus all classes that were affected by the oprichnina
underwent economic disruption. Willingly or unwillingly,
they traded their settled way of life for a mobile, if not
nomadic, way of life. The stability of the population
earlier achieved by the government was now lost through
the fault of that very government.
     Secondly, the inspection of ownership rights of
princes and boyars and the transfer of disgraced people
to new lands could have been done with the same degree
of calmness with which in later years (for example, under Tsar Feodor Ivanovich in 1593-1594) the landowning
rights of monasteries were reviewed, even though monastery lands were at times confiscated. But Ivan had found
it necessary to link this operation with political terror,
executions, the disgrace of individuals and whole families,
and devastation of the homesteads of princes and entire
towns and districts. As the oprichnina developed, the
state began to experience civil warfare and yet could not
discern the reason for this warfare. For the Tsar was
hunting enemies who did not resist him.
     There is no need to recount in detail the persecutions

and executions that contemporaries more than once have described in every startling particular. The historian N.M. Karamzin has recorded "six eras of executions" during the years 1560-1577. Later historians, however, have treated the matter more properly by viewing this entire period a single, unbroken epoch of murder. Not content with the destruction of the nobility alone, Ivan vented his wrath upon people of all walks of life and put them to death in great numbers. There exists, for example, a brief chronicle account of how in 1574 "the Tsar executed in Moscow, on the Prechistaia Square of the Kremlin, many boyars, the Archimandrite (Evfimy) of the Chudov Monastery, an archpriest and many people of all kind." In 1570 the Tsar went on a campaign against Novgorod. He departed from Aleksandrovskaia Sloboda in December of the preceding year and sacked towns along the way (such as Klin and Tver). Several weeks he spent in Novgorod, torturing and killing people by the hundreds and even by the thousands. If the incredible figure of 60,000 victims recorded in the chronicle cannot be accepted, we must accept the testimony of the Tsar's "synodal" (the book in which the names of the dead were recorded, to be remembered at Mass) that in Novgorod 1,505 men were "separated" (that is, put to death). Men of that day recalled the Tsar's visitation with horror. They said that because of him "Novgorod the Great became desolate" and that "because of him many people began to look like beggars and wandered about foreign lands."[12] The area around Novgorod also suffered, and Pskov experienced some torment, although this city merely witnessed pillage and not executions.

Not content with victimizing boyars and common people, Ivan lightly and readily exterminated members of the clergy. He even exiled and ordered killed Philip, the Metropolitan and head of the national Church, a man whom

Ivan himself had forced to agree to become metropolitan.
Prince Vladimir Andreevich Staritsky, whom the "chosen
council" had intended as Ivan's successor, likewise perished.
The result of this insane and generally unnecessary
terror was the complete derangement of the domestic life
of Muscovy. The aristocracy, exhausted but not quite an-
nihilated, along with its feeling of fear nourished bitter
hatred toward "the ancient blood-drinking clan" of the
Muscovite sovereigns and looked forward with anticipation
to its early end. At the close of 1579 Kurbsky, celebrating
Bathory's victory over Ivan, prophesied in a letter to Ivan
that, in the words of the psalms, "those who use their
throne to create lawlessness will not remain long in God's
sight" and that "those who gorge themselves on Christian
blood will soon vanish with all their household." Ivan's
health, already broken by his orgies, and his lack of grand-
children, could have suggested to Kurbsky that the "blood-
drinking clan" was dying out. The same hope for a quick
end to the tyrant must have been the consolation of still
others who were persecuted, among whom the Muscovite
dynasty had savage enemies.
This dream came true. Before a quarter of a century
had passed following Ivan's death, descendants of the persecuted princes seized the Muscovite throne through the
princes Shuisky. They immediately clashed with the Go-
dunovs and the Romanovs, who then represented the relatives by blood and marriage of Ivan's family, which had
died out. Other strata of the populace were no less bitter
than the boyars. The oprichnina and the terror turned all
people against "their" cruel authority and at the same time
introduced dissension into society. In the accurate observations of the Englishman, Giles Fletcher, who was in Moscow soon after Ivan's death, Ivan's base policies and bar-
baric actions had so shaken Muscovy and aroused such

general dissatisfaction and implacable hatred that matters could end only in a general uprising. This observation, made before the Time of Troubles, found full justification in subsequent events in Russia.

5 DISPLACEMENT OF THE WORKING CLASSES AND ECONOMIC CRISIS

The government first noticed disorder among the Muscovite people about the year 1570, but this disorder had of course begun earlier. Presumably it was occasioned, first, by the strenuous efforts of the authorities to regulate the system of service land tenure and, secondly, by the conquest of Kazan. Both occurred in the 1550s. We have pointed out in their proper place the procedures adopted regarding the standards of service demanded in return for service estates, the settlement of a full thousand servitors on service tenure estates in the vicinity of Moscow, and the general census of service and tax-paying lands in order better to calculate services and payments. All these actions increased the burdens imposed on the people by the government and encouraged emigrations to new and more desirable places. And better places did exist, in the newly conquered Volga region. Settlers were lured there by the rich soil, abundance of water and forest and unbounded room for settlement, tillage and business. Needing garrisons for the new towns it had founded, the government invited to the Middle Volga "immigrants from the upper reaches," from the Oka and the Upper Volga. The administration distributed lands in the Volga region to service people and clergy in order to strengthen the Russian element in the region, and these landholders brought with them to their new homesteads a work force drawn from the ancient center of the

Great Russian state. At the same time the road from the Oka and the Volga was opened past Nizhni Novgorod through the lands of the Cheremisy and the Votiaki[13] to the Viatka, then further to the Urals, long known in Great Russia for riches. Masses of people moved eastward and northeastward, partly encouraged in their migration by their civil authorities.

But not only the Volga region enticed people from their native Muscovite districts. The "Wild Field," which lay to the south of Riazan, Tula and Kaluga and hitherto had remained unsettled, beckoned to them. This region was used by Russian and Tatar wanderers, who found there refuge from the tyranny of enemies and sanctuary from the law, or else sought their livelihood from hunting or booty by pillaging Russian and Tatar frontier settlements. By the middle of the sixteenth century the Russians had become predominant on the "Wild Field." Calling themselves "Cossacks," they roamed without hindrance by the Tatars over the vast expanse that reached to the Northern Donets and the Lower Don. On the banks of the "steppe" rivers they erected their hunting "camps" and "felt tents" [*iurty*], where they lived by hunting and fishing. But there was better business to be found in the "Wild Field." Military pursuits were more attractive. Once having formed a military detachment, called a *stanitsa*, and having chosen an "ataman," they could go south to the Black Sea and obtain "homespun coats" in the Tatar and Turkish settlements. On the steppe roads, the *shliakhi*, that ran from Muscovy to the south, they could rob Russian and foreign merchants and even ambassadors from the Tsar and the Khan. Finally, when summoned by the Tsar, they could hire themselves out to state service and join the Muscovite army in special detachments. In this manner men followed each other into the "Wild Field," abandoning the state Ivan had terrorized; for the oprichnina and the burdens of the Livonian War had made it impossible for them to continue to live in Russia.

This emigration from Muscovy to the "Wild Field" did not seem to disturb the government at first. Ivan's contemporaries felt that he even encouraged this exodus to the south, in order to "fill the borders of his land with military men and thereby strengthen frontier forts against the enemy." One writer of this period has even commented that if "any vile creature who had committed evil acts and was sentenced to death could escape to the forts of the steppe or the region of Seversk," there he could escape "from death." But with the passage of time the consequences of this sort of indulgence began to disturb the Muscovite authorities. They then concluded that the diversion of people from Muscovy's heartland to the Volga region and the "Wild Field" would have a dire effect upon conditions at the core of the state.

By the 1570s the economic situation at the center of Muscovy had become critical. The outflow of population created in those areas an economic void because of a lack of workers. The cadasters remarked about the very many "barren places that once were villages," deserted patrimonial estates overgrown with forests, villages abandoned by their inhabitants, their churches "without singing," and arable lands left fallow without cultivation. In some places the memory of departed lords remained alive and wastelands still bore their names. But elsewhere the masters were already forgotten and "there was no one to find their names." Wherever the state of affairs in the vicinity of Moscow can be calculated numerically, striking figures emerge. Land surveys demonstrate that by the time of Ivan's death the thirteen *stany*[14] of the Moscow district comprised not over 135,000 acres of arable land. Of this,

as many as 43,200 acres (in round numbers) lay fallow on
service and patrimonial estates and, in addition, as many as
10,800 acres were taken off the tax rolls because of the absence of their owners. Thus as much as forty per cent of
the arable land was no longer performing its normal economic function. The remaining sixty per cent (that is,
81,000 acres) were divided as follows: 31,050 acres belonged to service and patrimonial masters and 49,950 acres
belonged to monasteries. Hence, by the end of Ivan's reign
the service people of the Moscow district left fallow almost
two-thirds of the arable land they could have overseen.
They maintained 31,050 acres but abandoned 54,000.

Still more dismal information is available at this time
from the provinces of Novgorod that lay near the theater
of the Livonian War. Here one estimate concludes that
only seven and one-half per cent of all arable land was
under cultivation, while ninety-two and one-half per cent
lay fallow. Information is lacking concerning the percent-
age of the populace that left the central districts of the
state for the frontiers, or the number of those who went
to any given place. We have only an "estimation" that
during the last years of the sixteenth century not less than
20,000 people left for the "Wild Field" and that these
swelled the ranks of older emigrants from Muscovy. This
figure, of course, hardly approximates the scope of this
outflow. Its true dimensions can be appreciated from the
fever that gripped proprietors and landowners in their struggle for labor forces at the end of Ivan's reign. Using all
means legal or illegal, seemly or improper, they tried to
retain on their farms the labor force that was slipping away
and worked to hold their peasants and slaves in their service while striving to obtain others from different sources.
Through peaceful transactions and court actions, as well
as with violence and deceit, they kept their own people

on their land and bound to themselves those who were
free, as well as men from other farms. The "carting off"
of peasants and the redemption and transfer of indebted
peasants became the source of constant conflict among
landowners. Rich, strong and clever landlords "exported"
to their lands under any pretext imaginable peasants who
belonged to poor, weak or less adroit landlords. Similarly,
they enticed non-agricultural workers, who entered "into
the household" of rich and generous lords "to serve them
willingly" in bondage. In reality these workers did not
serve "willingly" but because of deception and dire need.
To quote one contemporary, some fell into bondage "and
assumed obligations through force and torture, while others
were merely asked to drink some wine, and after three or
four cups they found themselves slaves in captivity against
their will."

The contest for laborers was won, of course, by the
influential and rich landowners (and most often by the
monasteries, which had at their disposal financial capital
and ties with Moscow). But this competition injured
both the peasantry and the petty servitors who held service tenure estates. Their peasants were the first to fall
into economic slavery, while the service men, having lost
their peasants, came to ruin and could no longer render
service from their lands. In both instances the government was the loser. The ruined peasant fled or sank into
slavery and consequently paid no taxes. The ruined landholder not only found it impossible to render service but
also "wasted" his official service estate and destroyed its
economic value. It was therefore unavoidable that the
government should intervene in this matter. In 1580 Ivan
extracted from a "consecrated council" and its head, Metropolitan Antony, a solemn promise that in the future
monasteries and other ecclesiastical landowners would

acquire no new lands or hold lands in mortgage, because
the "military class has suffered impoverishment from it."
Probably about this time the sovereign's "decree" appeared which said that peasants should not be carted off by
force and that in general peasants were not to be moved
about for a certain period of time "during forbidden years,"
which would be determined in advance by the government.
Unfortunately, the exact text of this "decree" by Ivan is
not preserved. But it did exist and was essentially the first
formal and provisional limitation upon the peasant's right
to leave his master, a freedom that hitherto had been recognized by Muscovite legislation.

6 THE STRUGGLE AGAINST THE CRISIS: THE SOUTHERN BORDERLANDS

The political terror and the depopulation of the central
districts of the state brought the Muscovite tsardom to
a domestic crisis of extraordinary magnitude. The long
war, the raids mounted by the Tatars in 1571 and 1572
and the crop failures that accompanied those years further aggravated this crisis. Ivan faced a grave and intricate problem. The land refused to give the government
the men and the means to continue the war. Because of
the rapid dispersal of the populace, the country generally
lost the resources needed to support the government. The
authorities had to repair the disorder and seek new means
of restoring the strength of the state. It was natural that
the political leadership should seek these resources in the
lands to which the laboring force had fled and attempt
to reenlist these forces in state service and satisfaction of
obligations they had avoided by flight.
    As far as the Volga region was concerned, the process

of settlement had proceeded under the eye and even under
the direction of Muscovite officials. For this reason the
registration of labor forces and resources on the whole
was accomplished conveniently and efficiently. As early
as the mid-1560s, after the confiscated Tatar lands were
distributed to Russian owners, the general registration of
lands began in the "Tsardom" of Kazan. The cadasters
recorded crown lands, service tenure estates of people
"who had been given a service rank," tenantless lands and
lands "which of old had belonged to the Tatars and Chuvash and Mordvinians and which were now suitable for dis-
tribution as service tenure lands." In one way or another
all registered lands fell under official control and were considered when services and payments were apportioned.

But matters were arranged differently in the south,
in the "Wild Field." At the beginning of the sixteenth
century the frontier of permanent Muscovite settlement
advanced from the Oka River ("from the bank," as it
was said at the time) to the fortified "line," which meant
the stone fortresses of Kaluga, Tula and Zaraisk. The central authorities strengthened and guarded this line, which
was garrisoned and reinforced by natural and artificial
"fortifications" against Tatar raids. Attentive to the smal-
lest detail, the government took care to be "more wary"
and ordered extreme watchfulness. But in the meantime,
despite the danger along the entire expanse of the fortified
frontier, the agricultural and commercial segments of the
population pressed forward ever farther to the south.
Without permission and even without the knowledge of
the authorities these people settled "on new lands," in
occupations of every kind. Their thrust outward was so
dynamic that the more enterprising among them even
settled beyond the limits of the fortresses, where the set-
tler was no longer protected by the moats, walls and

ramparts of towns but only by natural "fortifications"—
thickets or the current of tree-lined brooks. People of
this sort escaped all official notice and were quite lost to
the state. It was impossible to record them in the cadasters or to subject them to any kind of service or tax.
Meanwhile the needs of the government became ever more
acute and by 1571 Moscow had definitely resolved that
action should be taken to deal with the problem of the
southern frontier. News of the Tatar raids of 1570 provided the immediate impetus for doing so.

In January of 1571 the sovereign resolved "to construct stations and guard detachments," that is, to put
in order and improve the network of mounted sentry patrols and stationary observation posts that had long extended along the southern frontier but now was considered inadequate. The enterprise was entrusted to a boyar,
Prince Mikhail I. Vorotynsky. He summoned from the
southern towns to Moscow people experienced in out-
post duty and "who were already accustomed (to guarding the border) for ten or fifteen years." These people
"from all the frontier towns, *deti boiarskie*, long patrol
riders, short patrol riders[15] and guides [*vozhi*], should all
come to Moscow in January or in February." With them
Vorotynsky perfected a plan for early warning posts on
the frontier, by which the security line was extended from
Tula south to the Bystraia Sosna River and to Orel and
Briansk. Much of the expanse of the "Wild Field" thereby became part of Muscovite territory.

This was the manner in which the government colonized the "Wild Field," with a plan that was technically
devised very assiduously and in great detail. Since the
course of this special work gave rise to administrative
questions that went far beyond the jurisdiction of Vorotynsky's special commission, these problems were referred

to the boyar *duma*, where they were discussed and resolved
by special "decisions" made by the boyars. The matter
dragged on for several years. Vorotynsky was replaced by
the boyar Nikita R. Yuriev. The time-table by which the
"stations and guard detachments" were to be positioned
was altered more than once to conform to the advance
ever farther southward on the "Wild Field" of military and
isolated agricultural settlements. In Moscow officials devoted ever greater attention to the task of colonizing the
"Wild Field." At the end of Ivan's reign and during the
first years of the reign of his successor, Feodor Ivanovich,
the problem of incorporating the "Field" within the sphere
of governmental authority became paramount.

The dominant idea behind all the actions taken to
solve this problem was the realization that it was necessary to build fortresses on the "Field," to control and
close all fords across the rivers on Tatar routes from the
south to the Oka River—"to establish forts on the fords
along the Tatar routes." Thereafter it would be impossible for large Tatar forces to move secretly about the
steppe. To counter raids by smaller Tatar detachments,
various types of "fortresses," from "barriers of felled
trees" in the forests to ramparts and moats in the plains,
were created between the towns. All this formed an unbroken line of fortifications, beyond which permanent
sentry posts (the "guard detachments") and mounted patrols (the "stations") kept watch. The network of fortresses that was conceived in Ivan's day and implemented
by him and his successor enclosed the huge expanse of
the "Wild Field" between the Don River, the Upper Oka
and the left tributaries of the Dnepr and Desna rivers.[16]
This territory represented a distinctive conquest by Moscow, for the object of this conquest was neither enemy
towns nor an alien people but desolate places and people

of one's own nationality. Indeed, the intention was to
prevent the enemy from entering this conquered region.
For this purpose towns were built and an effort launched
to bind to these towns the local Russian settlers who had
abandoned Muscovy's central provinces and had crossed
the line of Russian settlement.

The Muscovite general who was sent to the "Field"
to found a new town arrived at the place where he had
been ordered to build the town and began his work. He
gathered information "along the brooks" of the presence
of free homesteaders[17] in those parts. Whenever he learned of the existence of free inhabitants, he invited them
to visit him and commanded "the ataman and the wealthy
Cossacks from all the rivers to come to him in the town."
In the name of the sovereign he strengthened their control over their "settlements" (homesteads) and persuaded
them to serve the sovereign by defending the borders and
the new town. These individuals then comprised the service people of the new town. They were the government's
compensation for its loss of military forces caused by the
depopulation and ruin of the central districts of the realm.

But this was not the limit of the responsibilities of
the free inhabitants who were now forcibly reincorporated
into the state by the official colonization of the "Field."
In each new district of the "Field" farming for the government was demanded; this was the so-called "tithe of arable
land cultivated for the state," which all minor military men
in the towns (with the exception of the *deti boiarskie*)
were obliged to plow along with their own lands. The
"tithe of arable land cultivated for the state" was needed
to replenish the state granaries, from which grain was distributed for various needs. This grain provisioned the men
of the garrison, who did not have their own farms. Government grain was also sent to towns farther to the south,

where agriculture had not yet been initiated, and was even
sent to the Don Cossacks as a form of "salary from the
Sovereign." In this manner the government planned to
compensate for the losses in agricultural products that were
the natural consequence of the economic crisis within Muscovy.

Concerns for the settlement and fortification of the
Volga region, especially of the southern frontiers of Muscovy, and concerns for the organization of the military
and laboring populace in these regions were the main goal
of governmental activity during the last years of Ivan's
reign. As the authorities scaled down the forceful repres-
sion of the oprichnina, they devoted correspondingly greater attention to organizing the frontiers which had been
part of the zemshchina. The researcher who limits his observations of Russian life during this period to the legislative activities of the central organs of authority will have
to recognize that these institutions accomplished nothing
and that Ivan dragged out his days in a dismal mood, suffering painful military reverses and at times surrendering
to fits of savage bitterness. Yet the slightest acquaintance
with the special historical materials that deal with the establishment of services and labor in the newly settled frontiers of the state afford an understanding of where the interests of the government were directed. These concerns
did not require general legislation and were limited to detailed implementation of a practical plan that had been
adopted. Although the activity of the government is not
reflected in laws and decrees, this work testifies to the
courage and viability of the government as much as had
the broad reforms of the early years of Ivan's life or the
impetuous venture of the oprichnina.

7 IVAN'S LAST YEARS

Ivan's most notable literary works date from the second
half of his reign, from the time of the oprichnina, the
war with Lithuania and Sweden and the organization of
the southern frontiers. Among these were his "very long"
epistle in response to Kurbsky's first letter in 1564, his
testament of 1572, his message to the Kirillov Monastery
in 1573 and the letters and official charters apparently
composed by the Tsar himself (the charters to King John
of Sweden and to Bathory, his letter to V.G. Griazny,
and so forth). Two features characterize Ivan's literary
style. First, he is unusually verbose and given to gracing
his own stylistic lavishness with meandering citations from
books he had read ("whole paragraphs and passages," to
quote Kurbsky). Secondly, Ivan greatly appreciated any
sort of banter, from good-natured irony to the bitterest
sarcasm, and loved to mock his correspondents in a snide
manner, opportunely or irrelevantly introducing clownish
elements into serious discourse.

   There is no need to dwell upon analysis of all these
works by Ivan, for they have been evaluated many times
by our historians and have become highly renowned. For
our purposes it should be noted that, regardless of how
one evaluates the literary qualities of these writings, they
testify that their author retained his intellectual powers
until the last years of his life and that Ivan's writings can
in no way be considered ravings of a madman or nonsense
of a stupid individual. Always they express a definite
theme, logically developed. There is constancy of thought
and clarity of feeling. Generally they show sense and wit.
But apart from all this, these works contain valuable

material for determining the feelings that motivated Ivan
during the most decisive moments of his life.

    More than once we have remarked that Ivan feared
the "chosen council." Apparently this feeling was sincere and deep. Ivan believed that he was under the power of his advisers, that their "council of dogs" commanded
all things, leaving him solely the honor of "presiding and
reigning," and that his family and his person were threatened with danger from these "cunning slaves" and "the
priest" who directed them. When finally he overcame this
fear and resolved to disperse the dangerous "council," he
sank into cowardice of another sort. Ivan surmised that
his rift with his former favorites had impelled them to re-
sort to "treason" and to harbor evil intentions toward
him. Yet in truth it was not they, but he who attacked
and persecuted those who opposed him or those whom
he found suspicious. But it seemed to Ivan that they had
attacked him and that he had to "stand by himself" and
protect himself. This aura of fear and his urge to defend
himself pervades all of Ivan's "widespread and very noisy
letters" to Kurbsky. From the Tsar's point of view, the
institution of the oprichnina was a necessary measure of
self-defense.

    Whenever Ivan raged against "traitors," he displayed
this attitude of a man oppressed and endangered. His testament of 1572 clearly reflects this state of mind. Even
while he was authoritatively disposing of his "treasury"
and all of his "Russian Tsardom," Ivan presented the image of one sorely beset by enemies. "I have been banished by the boyars, because of their willfullness, from my
possessions, and now I wander about my lands," he wrote.
By the words "my possessions" he meant the capital, and
by the word "lands" he meant those places where he lived
with his "court." In his later testament of 1582, which has

not come down to us, this strange passage has a different
reading. Those who lived in the eighteenth century and
saw the testament of 1582 report that the Tsar "speaks
more clearly of these things and forbids revenge; his wan-
dering means that he was pleased to live in Staritsa and
was even more pleased to live in Aleksandrovskaia Sloboda." Yet even in this version, which is not as strange as
the testament of 1572, the words "banished by boyars"
as used by the tyrant seem psychologically abnormal.
  This impression is strengthened by the consistency
with which Ivan represents himself and his children as
being banished and oppressed. "May God have mercy
and bring you to your kingdom and keep you there,"
Ivan wrote to his children, "and I bless you." In another place Ivan says: "May God have mercy on you, free
you from troubles, and may you never be separated."
Even in his well-known epistle to the Kirillov Monastery,
which is brimming with accusations against the monks,[18]
we can perceive again the attitude of one who is in danger.
Moreover, Ivan's third marriage to Marfa Sobakina[19] resulted in the death of many of her relatives. In a letter Ivan
recalls Varlaam Sobakin, the uncle of Marfa, who was consecrated a monk, and says of him that "Varlaam's nephews wished to torment me and my children with the help
of sorcery, but God hid me from them. Their sorcery
was discovered, and for this reason it happened" (that is,
they were executed). History knows nothing of any conspiracy or attempt against Ivan by the Sobakins; Ivan
alone reveals this apparently imaginary danger posed him
by this unfortunate family.
  Ivan's feeling of fear before non-existent danger reveals elements of the persecution mania that is so well
known and so widespread in our own times. As happens
among those suffering (or having) this mania, it did not

develop into a clearly defined mental illness in Ivan's case.
Until the end of his days Ivan continued to perceive impressions properly, well understood the complex picture
of political life and wisely addressed himself to its demands.
But at certain moments he would lose mental equilibrium,
easily surrender to fear and suspicion and fiercely defend
himself against imaginary threats and attacks. It was against
this background that the oprichnina developed, with all its
violence and executions, and the Tsar began to wander
"about my lands," instead of remaining settled in Moscow.
And, as is typical among those who undergo this mania,
the talkativeness and the inclination to joking and mock-
ery that is so characteristic of Ivan simultaneously emerged.

During the last active years of his life Ivan was no
madman. Rather, he was a man deprived of peace of mind
and haunted by fear for himself and those close to him.
This was one dimension of his "abnormality." Another,
which was related to the first, was his so-called "sadism,"
his blending of cruelty and depravity. This feature of
Ivan's nature had been fostered by his unfortunate childhood and grew to extreme proportions in old age. His
victims perished in refined tortures and died hundreds at
a time, for the sight of blood and torments gave the tyrant distinct satisfaction. At times Ivan "repented," ac-
knowledging that "he was corrupt of reason and beastly
of mind," that he defiled himself by murder, lechery and
every kind of evil act, that he was "like the foulest and
vilest corpse." But this was merely ritual.

Ivan sincerely and deeply repented and mourned only
when, in a fit of anger, he killed with his staff his own son.
Tsarevich Ivan was his father's sole hope of continuing
the clan, one who in all certainty would have continued
his father's policies and ruled with the same temper. Only
at the moment that he smashed his own future, so to speak,

did Ivan experience true grief and learn what it means to suffer. In his urgent dispatch from Aleksandrovskaia Sloboda to the boyars in Moscow on November 12, 1581, Ivan wrote that he was unable to come to Moscow, because the Tsarevich "has fallen sick and is now fatally ill." This dispatch is an eloquent testimonial to the mental disarray that overcame Ivan throughout the days that followed his unintentional crime. Yet soon after the Tsarevich died, Ivan recovered and returned to business. This was the time of the important and urgent negotiations with Bathory concerning peace, and there was no time for grief.

But during those gloomy years Ivan's intellectual life and work were not spent totally in vile exhibitions of cruelty and cynicism. Until the day of his death Ivan carried with him the good lessons he had learned from the "chosen council," such as its ability to organize broad administrative measures and its aptitude for implementing these measures practically and systematically. However one judges his personal conduct, Ivan, as a statesman and a politician, remains a distinguished figure.

In concluding this account of Ivan's activities during the second half of his reign, we must mention one tendency noted and censured by his contemporaries. This was his disposition toward foreigners and his interest in Western Europe. At the beginning of this essay it was noted that intercourse with Europe was a tradition in Ivan's family. Both his grandfather and his father had begun and maintained relations with the governments of Central and Southern Europe. The subjugation of Novgorod and Pskov made Russia the close neighbor of the "Northern European" Livonians and the Swedes and through them also of the Hanseatic League. The marriage alliance with the Paleologos family attracted to Russia representatives of the Latin nations, especially Italians. Ivan himself was the first to

initiate relations with England. The Livonian War brought
Ivan a certain relationship with Denmark, when it was
found that they had common enemies.
    Ivan was interested in more than the political and
commercial alliances that emerged from these various dealings. He was also curious about the culture of Europe, its
technology, its science and its religion. Earlier we have remarked how, soon after Moscow first became acquainted
with military mining, a specialist in mining, a "sapper,"
appeared before Kazan in Ivan's company, along with his
students. Mentioned also was Hans Schlitte, who recruited all varieties of specialists for Russia throughout Central
Europe. Ivan was also interested in physicians. Schlitte
invited to Russia more than twenty German members of
the medical profession. Those recruited in this manner
were unable to make their way to Ivan through the customs gates of the Hanse and Livonia. For this reason
other physicians freely entered Russia through the mouths
of the Northern Dvina and Kholmogory. These were Eng-
lishmen for the most part, and among them were people
who were indeed adept at their skills, such as Robert Jacob
and Arnold Lenzei.[20] There also appeared in Moscow in
1570 a graduate of Cambridge who was German in origin,
the doctor and astrologer ("sorcerer") Elisaeus Bomel, or
Bomely. This rogue and intriguer was destined to play a
prominent role during Ivan's day. For an entire decade
he attended the Tsar not only as a physician but also as
a fortune teller, astrologer and a maker of poisons that
were meant for those who fell into Ivan's disfavor. Contemporaries knew of his intimacy with the Tsar and found
it distressing. They even conjectured that Bomel had been
sent to Ivan by his enemies, the Lithuanians and Livonians,
saying that they "sent him a foreigner, a fierce sorcerer
named Elisaeus, who was close to and favored by the Tsar

and caused the Tsar to fear him . . . . He led the Tsar
away from the faith at last and caused him to become
vicious toward the Russian people and to love foreigners." So said one chronicle. Another contended that
Bomel really robbed Ivan of his senses. The Tsar, in the
words of this chronicle, "went off on campaigns and
wars and made his own land desolate; and because of
this unbeliever (Bomel) Ivan's mind became frenzied and
he intended to destroy the land, if the Lord had not ended his life." Although Bomel was finally put to death by
Ivan for the same reason that Ivan executed many of his
favorites—on suspicion of "treason"—nevertheless his influence upon the Tsar sank deeply into the memory of
the Russian people.[21]

One writer of the beginning of the seventeenth century, Ivan Timofeev, more clearly than other contemporaries put forth the idea that by the end of his life Ivan sympathized with foreigners and had succumbed to their influence. Timofeev said that the Tsar, after slaughtering some
of his boyars and driving others away, "began to love those
who had come to him from neighboring countries." Some
of these he made his intimate advisers ("privy to his secret
thoughts"); to others he entrusted his health, because of
their "wisdom in doctoring." But they brought "harm to
his soul, as well as ill health to his body," and in addition
filled Ivan with "hatred of his people." Timofeev thought
that even people of average intelligence should have understood that "one should never accept the faith of one's
enemies." But in the meantime Ivan "with such great wisdom was overcome by no one, except by the weakness of
his own conscience," and placed himself in the hands of
foreigners. "Alas," Timofeev exclaims, "his entire soul
was in the hands of barbarians, who did with him whatever they wished." Here Timofeev first and foremost

remembers Bomel, but he refers generally to the foreigners who, by the end of Ivan's reign, were appearing in the Muscovite state in considerable numbers. English and Dutch merchants who traded in Moscow and in the Russian North; captured northern Europeans and Lithuanians who were settled in various towns as far away as Laishev; foreign ambassadors who came to Moscow with large retinues—all these people could create the impression that the Tsar was conferring power upon the foreign element in Russia and protected and encouraged it.[22]

Rejecting the inescapable exaggerations, we shall not follow the chronicles and repeat that Ivan was deprived of his senses "by one who was non-Orthodox." But we must acknowledge that he was clearly and strongly inclined to have contact with Europeans and the West. There can be no doubt that during moments of "fear" of "treason" Ivan even considered the possibility of leaving Russia and at those times desired to seek sanctuary in the West, in England.[23]

NOTES

CHAPTER I: IVAN THE TERRIBLE IN RUSSIAN HISTORIOGRAPHY

1. Mikhail Mikhailovich Shcherbatov (1733-1790) published his *History of Russia from the Earliest Times* in seven volumes that appeared between 1770 and 1791. His work was significant not only in that it was the first historical study in Russia to rely upon primary sources but also because it did not limit its investigation to the person of the monarch, but studied the role of the nobility in the development of the Russian state. Robert Yurievich Wipper (Vipper) (1859-1954) was a Latvian monarchist who produced three editions of his work on the reign of Ivan IV. The first edition, written in 1922, was the version known to Platonov. Wipper's subsequent versions, composed during World War II, relished the return to strong centralized authority realized under Stalin.

2. The great fire of 1626 originated in the commercial city (Kitaigorod) and spread to the Kremlin, where it engulfed many buildings used by the government and the Church, destroying archival material and other treasures.

3. Nikolai Petrovich Likhachev (1862-1936) specialized in Russian documents of the sixteenth and seventeenth centuries, as well as genealogy, paleography and numismatics. His work on dating paper and watermarks was invaluable to the dating of Russian manuscripts.

4. N.P. Likhachev, *Delo o priezde v Moskvu Antoniia Possevina* (St. Petersburg, 1893), p. 60, table IV. (Platonov's note)

5. Prince Andrei Mikhailovich Kurbsky (1528-1583), to whom

Platonov refers repeatedly, was a close adviser and associate of Ivan the Terrible. In 1564 Kurbsky abandoned the armies he was commanding in Livonia and sought asylum in Lithuania-Poland, claiming that Ivan was preparing his execution. From Lithuania Kurbsky began a correspondence with Ivan and also composed his *History of the Great Prince of Moscow.* Most of Platonov's references to Kurbsky's writings intend the latter work, which has been translated into English and edited by J.L.I. Fennell, *Prince A.M. Kurbsky's History of Ivan IV* (Cambridge, 1965). As noted in the introduction to his work, the authenticity of all of Kurbsky's writings has been called into question.

6. Griazny-Il'in became one of Ivan's favorites after the Tsar's estrangement from Silvester and Adashev. Although Ivan's letters rebuked him for his stupidity in allowing himself to be captured by the Tatars, Ivan secured his release by paying the ransom demanded.

7. Petr Alekseevich Sadikov (1891-1942) studied under Platonov, then composed a study of Ivan IV's reign, *Ocherki po istorii oprichniny* (Moscow-Leningrad, 1950). Sadikov is best remembered, however, for his work on Russian history and literature of the nineteenth and twentieth centuries, concerning which he wrote more than twenty works.

8. The *litsevoi svod* is an illuminated manuscript created in Moscow in 1560-1570, comprising more than 10,000 pages with 16,000 miniatures. It surveys history from the creation of the world to the second half of the sixteenth century.

9. Johann Taube and Elert Kruse were Livonian nobles who were captured by the Muscovite army during the Livonian War. Because of their education and experience, Ivan made them his ambassadors to Livonia and Denmark and later entrusted them with a military command against Livonia. When their attack on Dorpat ended in failure, Taube and Kruse, fearing Ivan's displeasure, fled to Lithuania, where they wrote the above-mentioned letter on the persecution and terror mounted in Russia by the Tsar.

10. Giles Fletcher (1546-1611) served in Russia in 1588-1589 as an ambassador of Queen Elizabeth to the court of Ivan's successor, Feodor Ivanovich. His account of Russia, *Of the Russe Commonwealth*, is generally regarded the most important English description of affairs in Russia before the eighteenth century.

11. The term "boyar" designated members of the highest rank of the Muscovite service aristocracy. This title could be conferred on an individual only by the Tsar.

12. Although Ivan III had first used the title of Tsar, he had employed it only intermittently. Ivan IV began the customary use of this title, which now became perpetual.

13. In 1571 Prince Ivan F. Mstislavsky, one of Ivan's chief advisers and leading field commanders, confessed to having betrayed Moscow by aiding the Khan of the Crimea, Devlet-Girei, during an attack across the Oka River. It is possible that those decapitated in 1574 had been involved in this treachery. Mstislavsky himself had escaped death by pledging to refrain from future treason and by providing three boyars who were to stand surety for his future actions.

14. Nikolai Mikhailovich Karamzin(1766-1826), Russian historian and novelist. His *History of the Russian State* in twelve volumes was left unfinished at his death and records Russian history only until 1613. Often criticized for its romantic approach to history, this work remains important because of its citation of many sources later destroyed by fires and other disasters.

15. In an attempt to escape censorship and police harassment perpetrated by the regime of Nicholas I, the Slavophiles met in literary salons and circles in Moscow, where they discussed the many issues that later became part of their nationalistic ideology. Seeking a comprehensive system of thought to explain Russian greatness, they particularly studied the evolution of Russian institutions and the important roles played in world history by Russian rulers.

16. Konstantin Sergeevich Aksakov (1817-1860) was one of the most important and talented members of the Slavophile school and devoted much of his writing to history and philology. Yury Feodorovich Samarin (1819-1876), renowned for his poetry, also developed Slavophile ideas in a number of philosophical and historical essays and devoted much energy to writing of and working for the emancipation of the serfs.

17. Nikolai Ivanovich Kostomarov (1817-1885) was a Ukrainian historian, professor at the universities of Kiev and St. Petersburg and the author of many historical works.

18. Count Aleksei Konstantinovich Tolstoi (1817-1875) is the author of *The Death of Ivan the Terrible* and other works of historical fiction. His novel, *The Silver Prince*, is a vivid and exciting depiction of life in the days of Ivan IV.

19. Mark Matveevich Antokolsky (1843-1902) was a sculptor whose fidelity to historical detail and insight into the character of historical figures won him great renown. In 1870-1871 he produced in bronze the likeness of Ivan to which Platonov here refers. Ilia Efimovich Repin (1844-1930), the famous naturalist painter, produced his "Ivan the Terrible Kills His Son, Ivan" in 1885. Viktor Mikhailovich Vasnetsov (1848-1926), who often painted historical scenes and episodes from Russian epic poetry, produced a portrait of Ivan that hangs in the Tretiakov Gallery in Moscow.

20. Likhachev, *op. cit.,* pp. 62ff. (Platonov's note)

21. Sergei Mikhailovich Soloviev (1820-1879) was professor of history at the University of Moscow. His *History of Russia from the Earliest Times* in 29 volumes is renowned as the most ambitious history of Russia ever produced.

22. Appanage *(udel)* was the term used to denote land held by independent Russian princes during the thirteenth-sixteenth centuries. *Veche* was a meeting or assembly of townsfolk. In some

cities, such as Novgorod, the *veche* became powerful enough to determine the political life of the community. Both the appanage and
the *veche* were, as Platonov indicates, obstacles to the consolidation
of strongly centralized government.

23. Konstantin Dmitrievich Kavelin (1818-1885) was professor of
legal history at the University of Moscow and supported the view
that the Russian state was not of popular origin but had been impressed upon apathetic masses by strong and far-seeing individuals.
His historical views caused him to remain a staunch supporter of
monarchy during his own times.

24. Konstantin Nikolaevich Bestuzhev-Riumin (1829-1897) was
professor of history at the University of St. Petersburg. He dis-
avowed systematic interpretations of history and argued the role
played in historical development by strong individuals and for-
tuitous events and accidents.

25. Platonov's claim here is untenable today. Both the financial
system and the oprichnina are still subjects of controversy among
historians.

26. Russians of Ivan's day used the term the "Wild Field" to denote the vast, largely unpopulated steppe that extended beyond
the southern borders of the Muscovite state and separated Russian
territory from the lands of the Tatars.

27. The service people (*sluzhilye liudi*), of which the boyar class
was preeminent, were the servitors of the Muscovite government.
They were charged with rendering military, administrative and
other types of service for the state in return for compensation,
often in the form of landed estates.

28. Vasily Osipovich Kliuchevsky (1841-1911) is probably the
most respected historian of the Russian state. A great stylist and
popular lecturer at the University of Moscow, he pioneered the
sociological approach to the study of Russian history. His *Course*

in Russian History in five volumes treats Russian history until the reign of Nicholas I.

29. Metropolitan Macarius not only provided Ivan with a strong education but also urged him to reform the Church and morals in Russia, encourage literary pursuits and promote the power and majesty of the office of Grand Prince.

30. Service tenure land (*pomestie*) was land given servitors in return for service to the state. The holding of such land was conditional and could be revoked by the government if the service tenure landholder (*pomeshchik*) failed to render service.

31. Patrimonial land (*votchina*) was owned outright by its lord. Unlike *pomestie*, it could be willed to descendants without the approval of the central authorities.

32. *Deti boiarskie* (literally, "sons of the boyars") were a lower category of servitors in the Muscovite state. By the time of Ivan IV they bore much of the responsibility for rendering military service to the sovereign.

33. Aleksei Basmanov and Grigory Maliuta Skuratov were Ivan's close friends and collaborators during the oprichnina. Silvester will be identified in later chapters.

CHAPTER II: IVAN'S UPBRINGING

1. The extreme northwest section of Russia that adjoined the White Sea and the Arctic Ocean was known as the Pomorie.

2. The Cheremisy were a people of Finno-Ugrian origin who settled the northwestern section of European Russia during ancient times.

3. The Mordvinians were another Finno-Ugrian people whose homeland stretched along the Sura River, southwest of Kazan.

4. The Zavolochie section of Novgorod's settlements was the area that lay in the basin of the Northern Dvina River, north of Vologda and Ustiug.

5. Batu Khan led the Mongol invasion of Russia in the thirteenth century. Fear of later Mongol raids and punitive expeditions caused many Russians to migrate to new homesteads deeper in the forest zone, where forested wastes made Mongol incursions more difficult and less frequent.

6. The Russians called the territory liberated from the Khanate of Kazan the "Lower Reaches."

7. Sophia Paleologos, who married Ivan III in 1472, was the niece of the last Byzantine Emperor, Constantine XI. After the fall of Constantinople in 1453 she had converted to Catholicism and had lived in Rome as a ward of the Papacy until her marriage to Ivan.

8. Sophia was accompanied to Moscow in 1472 by a large contingent of courtiers, merchants, artists and churchmen who hoped to secure the reunion of the Latin and Orthodox churches, and other Westerners. Sophia was highly influential in introducing Moscow and its court to many aspects of Western and Byzantine culture, learning and manners.

9. The Grand Prince apparently adopted Western dress and certain Western customs. This imitation of the "heretical" Westerners seems to have been especially distasteful, if not scandalous, to native Russians.

10. Sviatopolk the Accursed (980?-1019) became Grand Prince of Kiev after a vicious civil war with his brothers, two of whom (the canonized saints Boris and Gleb) he put to death. He was said to have had "two fathers" because the chronicle records that his father, Vladimir, married his mother when she was already pregnant with Sviatopolk by another man.

11. Located forty miles northeast of Moscow, the Trinity-St. Sergius Monastery, one of the most important in Russia, was famous for its miracles and popular as a place of pilgrimage for Russian noblemen and common folk alike.

12. Wealthy Russians often undertook to build a church in a single day when seeking favors from God. The desire to have the supplication answered as quickly as possible probably accounts for the speed with which the building was erected.

13. The term *yurodivy* (plural, *yurodivye*) was used in Russia to designate obviously insane or half-witted holy men (the so-called "fools in Christ") who frequented public places or waited along roadsides to urge their fellow Christians to practice morality and cultivate devotion in their lives. Russians believed that the *yurodivy* had voluntarily surrendered his reason to God, in order to become a more perfect instrument of His grace.

14. The feast of the apostle Titus is celebrated on August 25, which was Ivan's birthday. Hence the meaning of the prediction. In the opinion of St. John Chrysostom, Titus was the most clever of St. Paul's disciples. Perhaps this explains the words "broad intellect." (Platonov's note)

15. That is, Vasily began to prepare a group of close and trusted advisers who would continue his policies and protect his family after his death.

16. Platonov here does not mean the so-called "boyar *duma*" but a council (*sovet*) of handpicked individuals. The *duma* (or boyar *duma*) was the council of prominent servitors who assisted the Tsar in matters of legislation, administration and foreign affairs.

17. A state secretary (*diak*; plural, *diaki*) was a functionary in the Muscovite civil service who often served as special assistant to the boyars, acted as an official in various departments of the government or occasionally was appointed head of a department of state. The state secretaries have been called the "mainspring of the Moscow bureaucratic apparatus." Many of them seem to have been of slave origin.

18. With the exception of Prince Andrei Mikhailovich Shuisky, who was imprisoned apparently for his role in the matter of the appanage Prince Yury. (Platonov's note)

19. After the political disintegration of the "Golden Horde," the large Mongol state that had dominated Russia from its capital at Sarai, three successor states emerged: the khanates of Kazan, Astrakhan and the Crimea. The Khanate of the Crimea, which became a vassal of the Ottoman Empire, was politically more viable and militarily stronger than the other two khanates and posed a constant threat to Russia until the Crimea was absorbed into the Russian Empire by Catherine II in 1783.

20. Apparently the kennel keepers believed that Ivan wished them to murder Shuisky privately. Because of a mistranslation of this account from contemporary sources, many American histories of Russia have stated erroneously that Shuisky was thrown to the hunting dogs at Ivan's command and was torn to pieces in their kennels. The Russian word in question is *psar'* (plural, *psari*) and was originally used to designate servants who maintained the dogs in households of princes and noblemen. By Ivan's day, however, the *psari* were high-ranking courtiers who probably had nothing to do with the keeping of dogs and their kennels.

21. The Glinsky family had brought a detachment of militia servitors from Severia to Moscow to protect themselves against the mobs of the city. Twice before smaller fires in the city had impelled the inhabitants to seek scapegoats among the Glinsky clan. For their part, the Glinsky family feared, seemingly with good cause, that their enemies were setting fires deliberately to cause them embarrassment and trouble.

22. In a letter to Kurbsky, Ivan recounts that the boyars poorly fed and clothed him and his brother, behaved impudently toward them ("Often I ate late, not by my own will") and insulted the memory of his father. They also stole public money, gold, silver and furs and "did everything for their own gain." These accusations were for the most part directed against the Shuisky clan. (Platonov's note)

23. The *Cheti Minei* (literally, Monthly Readings) compiled by Macarius consisted of twelve large volumes of devotional and instructional material so arranged that religious reading was provided for each day of the month.

24. A *namestnik* (plural, *namestniki*) was a local official appointed by the Grand Prince or Tsar to serve as local administrator and judge in towns and their surrounding districts. As Platonov will explain later, these officials provided for their own maintenance and expenses by revenue derived, sometimes excessively and forcibly, from the local community.

25. An *okol'nichii* (plural, *okol'nichie*) was, in central and eastern Russia, a courtier of high rank in the Muscovite service aristocracy who often received lofty military, diplomatic, judicial and administrative appointments.

26. This family later won historical greatness under the name of Romanov. It was customary for members of each generation of this family to change their last name, patterning it upon the first name of the grandfather. First known as the Koshkin family, the clan was successively called Yuriev, Zakharin and finally Romanov.

CHAPTER III: THE FIRST PERIOD: REFORMS AND THE
TATAR QUESTION

1. Kitai-gorod was the "Walled City" section of Moscow, directly east of the Kremlin. Its name derives from baskets, known as *kity*, which were filled with earth and used to reinforce the wall that surrounded this section. Here foreign merchants and traders had their markets and here much of the business of the city was conducted.

2. *Zamoskovie* (literally, the region beyond the Moskva River) was the term by which Russians designated the lands north and east of Moscow.

3. The intimate *duma* (*blizhniaia duma*) was the select group of high dignitaries upon whom the Tsar relied for the most personal and urgent advice. It can be contrasted with the *duma* "of all the boyars," which was the general session of all the Tsar's advisers.

4. We know the individuals who comprised the boyar *duma* of "all the boyars" and the intimate *duma* during those years. At that time the intimate boyars were Prince I.F. Mstislavsky, Prince V.I. Vorotynsky, I.V. Sheremetev "the senior," Prince D.I. Kurliatev, M.Ya. Morozov, Prince D.F. Paletsky and Daniel Romanovich Yuriev-Zakharin. Of these only Kurliatev belonged to the "chosen council." (Platonov's note)

5. According to Dal', a *batozhnik* was a servant with a *batog* (stick) who walked before the train of the Tsar or the boyars and cleared the way. In the North the word meant an ecclesiastical watchman with a stick (according to Dal'). (Platonov's note)

6. "Sochineniia kniazia A.M. Kurbskogo," *Russkaia Istoricheskaia Biblioteka*, XXXI, pp. 28, 30, 55. (Platonov's note)

7. The Rurikids were, of course, the descendants of Rurik, who founded the ruling Russian dynasty. The Gediminovichi were descendants of princes who had accepted the political control of the Grand Prince Gedimin (or Gedymin) of Lithuania, who ruled the Principality of Lithuania from 1316 until 1345 and added much Russian territory to his state.

8. That is, Ivan addressed a council of bishops and other eminent churchmen, at which prominent boyars were present.

9. This important information can be found in a little known chronicle which has not been reprinted with care (*Polnoe sobranie russkikh letopisei*, XXII, pp. 528-529). This event of February 27, 1549 apparently gave rise to the legend concerning the Assembly of the Land of 1547 or 1550, when the Tsar was alleged to have solemnly delivered on the square a penitential speech to all people, promising them justice (see Karamzin, *Istoriia gosudarstva rossiiskago*, VII, chapter III and notes 182 and 184). (Platonov's note)

10. These charters (*gramoty zhaloval'nye*) were probably the Tsar's official notification to the *deti boiarskie* that they would be immune from trial by the *namestniki*.

11. The Council was known as the *Stoglav* (Hundred Chapters) because its final pronouncements were issued in a work comprising one hundred chapters.

12. The first *Sudebnik*, or Code of Law, had been promulgated in 1497 and was largely a compilation of procedural rules. Ivan's *Sudebnik* of 1550 was much more ambitious and complex, dealing heavily with matters of local administration.

13. Elders (*starosty*) were esteemed men selected by local communities. Sworn men (*tseloval'niki*) were officials who were designated to attend the courts convened by *namestniki* to ensure that justice was done. They pledged their impartiality and devotion

to justice by kissing the cross; hence their title, which derives from the Russian word "to kiss." *Sotskie* were elected civil officials who served as judges or administrators in rural areas but whose main function was that of police. *Piatidesiatskie* were elected officials charged with preserving order in local communities. They received their name (which originates from the Russian word for "fifty") from their military counterparts, who commanded units of fifty men in the Muscovite army.

14. A dependent town (*prigorod*) was what we would today term a suburb, a smaller urban area administratively subordinated to a larger municipality.

15. The peasant communes (*volosti*) were communities that were semi-autonomous and administered by elected officers who regulated the use of common lands such as pastures, forests and sources of water, apportioned land to individual households and collected taxes and maintained law and order in the name of the sovereign.

16. Rural administrative districts (*pogosti*) were originally settlements in the North that contained at least one church, a marketplace and a cemetery (from which this term derives). By the end of the reign of Ivan IV the term meant fiscal and administrative units that had developed from these humble origins.

17. These charters (*ustavnye gramoty*) were patents of local self-government granted to communities by the Tsar upon petition.

18. In Ivan's day the *uezd* resembled the modern notion of a county, an administrative-judicial unit that centered about a municipality.

19. *Kormlenie* (literally, feeding) was the system by which *namestniki* supported themselves, in lieu of salary, by appropriating part of the court fees, taxes and other revenue paid by the local populace.

20. A rural chief (*volostel'*) was the counterpart of the *namestnik* in rural regions, overseeing the peasant communes and also supporting themselves through *kormlenie.*

21. *Kormy* (singular, *korm*) were specified payments, in kind or in money, demanded by *namestniki* for their maintenance. Customs duties (*poshliny*) were those revenues collected in compensation for providing any one of several official services for the local community. In theory, two-thirds of all funds collected by the *namestnik* were to be paid to the central government.

22. It was precisely this sort of plaintiff who came to the Tsar from Pskov to complain of Prince Turuntai-Pronsky and whom the Tsar brutally tormented in the village of Ostrovka during the spring of 1547. (Platonov's note)

23. These were assessors [*prisiazhnie*] who derived their title from the fact that they were made to "kiss the cross that they would gather their revenue and profits in justice and without guile." (Platonov's note)

24. Favorite elders (*izliublennye starosty*) were elected officials who acted as local governors and judges in the courts.

25. Favorite heads (*izliublennye golovy*) were officials of local administration who collected taxes levied by the state.

26. Judges of the land (*zemskie sudi*) were local judges elected by the local populace. As part of Ivan's reforms they now assumed the judicial functions previously held by *namestniki* and *volosteli.*

27. Elders of the court (*sudetskie starosty*) were locally elected judges.

28. The good men (*liudi dobrye*) were wealthy, respected and supposedly uncorruptable men who were named to serve as jurors or assistants in courts on days of trial.

29. The *guba* was, after Ivan's reforms, a criminal judicial district. The boundaries of each *guba* usually coincided with those of the local *uezd* (see note 19 of this chapter).

30. Provincial elders (*zemskie starosty*) were locally elected officers who were the administrative counterpart of the *zemskie sudi* in the judicial process (see note 26 of this chapter).

31. The district elder (*gubnoi starosta*) was an elected elder who served as criminal judge in his local district.

32. District office (*gubnaia izba*) designated the building in which offices of the district government were housed, as well as the entire apparatus of district government.

33. Town commissioners (*gorodovye prikashchiki*) implemented the decrees of the central authorities in their towns and oversaw arrests made by *namestniki* and *volosteli*, verifying their legality.

34. Census takers (*pistsy*) were common clerks who kept the census.

35. Census reviewers (*dozorshchiki*) kept the inventory of population and tax records, revised tax assessments and registered the ownership of lands and peasants.

36. *Mestnichestvo* was a highly complex system that determined the relative standing of each prince, boyar and servitor in the Muscovite court. Claims to service position were based upon each individual's place in this system. Thus the Tsar was constrained by custom to observe this hierarchy when appointing military commanders, administrators and other officials. This system lasted until 1682.

37. *Streltsy* (singular, *strelets*) were infantry armed with arquebuses who comprised the first permanent regiments of the Muscovite army. Created by Ivan the Terrible, these military units were exempt from taxation and lived in their own communes, where they were allowed to engage in trade, business and other lucrative occupations during their free time.

38. The three-field agricultural system came into use in Russia at the end of the fifteenth century and involved the rotation of crops across three plots of land in succession.

39. The *sokha* (literally, plow) was a territorial unit that encompassed tracts of farmland in rural areas and numbers of individual households in urban areas. The size of the *sokha* (plural, *sokhi*) varied according to the quality of farmland or the income and wealth of the townsfolk. For a clear definition of the limits of *sokhi*, see Richard Hellie, *Enserfment and Military Change in Muscovy* (Chicago, 1971), p. 125.

40. The *bol'shoi dvorets* was an institution that managed the extensive palace-owned lands and oversaw the taxing of their peasant population. The *bol'shoi prikhod* later assumed some of its responsibilities. The Taxation Chancelleries (*cheti*) were created during the oprichnina to collect revenues formerly paid to officials who had subsisted on *kormlenie.*

41. Evgeny Evsigneevich Golubinsky (1834-1912) was perhaps Imperial Russia's greatest historian of the Russian Church. His *History of the Russian Church* in two volumes is still considered the standard work on the subject.

42. The white clergy were the parish priests. Unlike the "black," or monastic, clergy they were allowed to marry. Their level of education was often very low and their moral lives little better.

43. Mohammed II, who was Ottoman Sultan from 1451 to 1481 and captured Constantinople in 1453.

44. That is, the Volga Bulgars who did not accompany their fellow tribesmen to their new homeland on the Danube but founded their own state in the Volga-Kama basin.

45. The *murzy* and *beki* were princely and aristocratic lords who wished to preserve their immunities and independence by contending for control of the Khanate of Kazan.

46. That is, the Khanates of Astrakhan and the Crimea.

47. That is, the Volga River became the dividing line between the territory that remained under the control of Kazan and that which now came under the jurisdiction of the Russians.

48. 2,700 Russian captives were at once surrendered to the boyars in Kazan. According to Muscovite calculations, 60,000 men returned to Russia from the Khanate of Kazan through Sviazhsk alone, going "up the Volga"—and this did not count those who returned by other routes by going to Viatka, Perm and Vologda—"all going to their own places, to those places that were close to them." (Platonov's note)

49. The Nogai Tatars were a tribe of independent Tatars who controlled the area east of the Lower Volga and the basin of the Yaik (Ural) River.

50. According to Kurbsky, Ivan's personal regiment, which he led in battle, numbered over 20,000 men.

51. Karamzin interpreted the word "Razmysl" as it was used in the chronicle as a common noun and explained that it meant a "foreign engineer." In the dictionaries of Dal' and Sreznevsky the word "razmysl" has several meanings, but none in the sense of "engineer." It is most likely that "Razmysl" is a corruption of the family name "Rasmussen." In 1602 the Danish envoy, Peter Rasmussen, was called "Petr Razmysl" in Moscow. (Platonov's note)

CHAPTER IV: THE PERIOD OF TRANSITION

1. If Yury had been capable, he would have been the main supporter of his nephew, Dmitry. But Yury was irresponsible. Kurbsky flatly says of him that "he was without mind, memory or speech and, strange as it seems, had been born so." Until his death in 1563 Yury is remembered for no accomplishment either in official records or in the chronicles. (Platonov's note)

CHAPTER V: IVAN'S FINAL PERIOD: THE BALTIC QUESTION AND THE OPRICHNINA

1. The Sech was the base of the Ukrainian Cossacks that developed during the second half of the sixteenth century on islands in the Lower Dnepr River.

2. Ataman was the title accorded military commanders elected by the various Cossack communities.

3. Russians often referred to the Khan of the Crimea as the "Khan of Perekop."

4. Although the first Pseudo-Dmitry had envisaged such a campaign against the Tatars of the Crimea, subsequent political developments within the Muscovite state prevented him from undertaking this enterprise.

5. In 1687 and 1689 Golitsyn attacked the Crimean Tatars on the steppe and suffered great reversals, largely because his forces suffered from lack of water and supplies and were exhausted from the long distances they had marched during these campaigns.

6. Burkhard Münnich was military adviser to Peter the Great, then commander of the Russian armies under the Empress Anne. In 1739 he led a Russian army that invaded Moldavia, captured Khotin, crossed the river Pruth and penetrated as far as Jassy.

7. In 1503 the Bishop of Dorpat had assumed an obligation to pay an annual tribute to the Grand Prince of Moscow.

8. The term "hetman" (which derived from the German Hauptmann) was the title by which the supreme commander of the military forces of Lithuania and Poland was known.

9. *Gosti* (singular, *gost'*) were the richest and most privileged rank of merchants in Russia. They received their title from the Tsar and served the government by collecting state revenue and regulating state commercial operations.

10. The Jagellonian dynasty ruled Poland, Bohemia, Lithuania and Hungary during the fourteenth to sixteenth centuries.

11. A pan (plural, pani) was a member of the feudal aristocracy of Poland and Lithuania. The pani held the most important positions of national and regional government and owned vast estates and large numbers of serfs.

12. The notion that Ivan caused 5,000 of the 6,000 inhabited households of Novgorod to become deserted must be abandoned. Novgorod quickly decreased in population because of the effects of the Livonian War. Yet there is no doubt that the massacre of 1570 claimed a great many victims and furthered the impoverishment of the region. (Platonov's note)

13. The Votiaki were a Finnish tribe of the Permian group living primarily in the southeastern part of the Viatka region.

14. *Stany* (singular, *stan*) were rural administrative units that were subdivisions of the *uezdy* in Muscovite Russia.

15. Long patrol riders (*stanichniki*) patrolled large areas of the steppe and alerted towns of impending danger. Short patrol riders (*storozhi*) rode about a smaller area and reported signs of danger to local control and observation posts.

16. The major fortified towns in this network were Briansk, Orel, Kromy, Novosil', Livny, Elets, Voronezh, Oskol and Kursk. (Platonov's note)

17. The Russian word for free settlers of this sort is *zaimshchiki*, which denotes individuals who occupied and cultivated previously unused land in uninhabited areas. Muscovite law recognized the right of ownership of such land by virtue of occupancy.

18. The Kirillov (St. Cyril) Monastery had been founded southeast of the town of Beloozero by St. Kirill at the end of the fourteenth century. The monks of this monastery drew the ire of the Tsar because of their great love for wealth, their neglect of religious and monastic duties and their immorality.

19. Marfa Sobakina died two weeks after her marriage to the Tsar. Three members of her family were executed and her uncle was banished by Ivan to a monastery. (Platonov's note)

20. Robert Jacob was an English physician whom Queen Elizabeth sent to Russia in 1581 at Ivan's special request. Arnold Lenzei was a Belgian doctor whose medical treatises were translated into Russian on orders of the Russian government.

21. On Bomel see S.F. Platonov, *Moscow and the West*, trans. and ed. by Joseph L. Wieczynski (Hattiesburg: Academic International Press, 1972), pp. 20-21; also Lloyd E. Berry and Robert O. Crummey, *Rude and Barbarous Kingdom* (Madison, 1968), pp. 292-293.

22. Here Platonov briefly summarizes many of the themes which he develops in his masterful study, *Moscow and the West*.

23. Ivan seems first to have considered the idea of seeking refuge in England in 1567, when he sent a secret message through Anthony Jenkinson to Queen Elizabeth, asking that each pledge asylum to the other in the event of a great domestic crisis. Elizabeth assured Ivan that "if any mischance might happen in his estate . . . we do assure him, he shall be friendly received into our dominions." Karamzin later affirmed that the idea of a flight to England was suggested to Ivan and promoted by Bomel, but there is no evidence for this contention. Indeed, Bomel first met the Tsar two years after Elizabeth's offer of sanctuary in England. Ivan's reason for considering emigration apparently was his fear that the oprichnina would create too many enemies for him to destroy.

Reconstruction by M.M. Gerasimov published January 1964 following exhumation on April 23, 1963

IVAN THE TERRIBLE

INDEX

Platonov, Sergei Fedorovich, 1860-1933.
  Ivan the Terrible [by] S.F. Platonov. Ed. and trans. by Joseph L.
Wieczynski. With "In search of Ivan the Terrible" by Richard Hellie.
[Gulf Breeze, Fla.] Academic International Press, 1974.
  xxxviii, 166 p. maps, ports. 22 cm. (The Russian series, v. 28)

  Translation of Ivan Groznyi.

  "Notes": p. 135-154.
  1. Ivan IV, the Terrible, Czar of Russia, 1530-1584. 2. Russia—
Hist.—Ivan IV, 1533-1584. I. Wieczynski, Joseph L., ed. and tr.
II. Hellie, Richard. In search of Ivan the Terrible. 1974.

DK106.P613   947.04'0924   77-176468
ISBN: 0-87569-054-8

THE RUSSIAN SERIES